IF THESE LIPS COULD TALK

IF THESE LIPS COULD TALK

By Frank Pace with Billy O'Connor

Acclaim Press
MORLEY, MISSOURI

Acclaim Press
—— *Your Next Great Book* ——

P.O. Box 238
Morley, MO 63767
(573) 472-9800
www.acclaimpress.com

Cover artwork by: Man One © 2020
Man One's award winning artwork has been exhibited at museums and galleries
internationally. His muralsand street art can be seen on city walls worldwide.
For more info visit: www.ManOne.com

ISBN: 978-1-948901-63-5 / 1-948901-63-3
Library of Congress Control Number: 2020939755

First Printing 2020
Printed in the United States of America
10 9 8 7 6 5 4 3 2 1

This publication was produced using available information.
The publisher regrets it cannot assume responsibility for errors or omissions.

TABLE OF CONTENTS

DEDICATIONS

Frank Pace
I once read that every time an old person dies,
it's as if a library burns down.

To my mother, Rose,
with whom I wished I had shared more of these stories.

To my wife, Karen and daughter Erin,
who lived through many of them.

To my granddaughter Frankie
who will now have access to a hefty portion of my life's library.

Billy O'Connor
To the 343 of my fallen Brothers who gave the ultimate sacrifice on
9/11, to the over 1,400 rescue workers who have died since, and to the
thousands more still battling life-threatening injuries.

To my family, to Alcoholics Anonymous, and to all teachers
everywhere.

I'll never forget.

FOREWORD

I have never played on a sports team, but if I had, I would have wanted Frank Pace as my coach. He's a true leader. He's the kind of person who protects and upholds the entire company yet has your back as an individual. He's quick with a laugh, challenges you to reach your potential, often offering an appropriate dose of tough love, and is always sensitive to the delicate balance that must be struck when working with a diverse group of people and personalities.

While doing a situation comedy, it isn't just about making TV … it's about intense work, deep commitment, preparedness for change, and loving what you do. In my life I have never been happier or freer than when I was under Frank's watchful eye, during *Suddenly Susan*. I had found my calling and my family, but also, have never been sadder or more imprisoned by loss. This book tells the truth of the behind the scenes of life on a sound stage. It is unique, funny, tender, shocking, and entirely enjoyable to experience. You will come away feeling satisfied by being told the truth, and by being invited to feel closer to those of us, who were lucky enough to have been on a team with its author.

*(Andrew Eccles / Alamy
Stock Photo)*

— Brooke Shields
Actress, Star of *Suddenly Susan*,
and *New York Times* Best-Selling Author

INTRODUCTION

By Billy O'Connor

"You know what, Frank? Go screw yourself. This is a great story."

I had just suggested that the co-executive producer of the Disney Channel's hit show *Shake It Up* go screw himself. Which is a bit odd considering I had come into his L.A. office looking for a favor and had only met him for the first time half an hour earlier.

It wasn't said maliciously.

Something about Frank's voice just made me feel comfortable. The way he said things, his mannerisms, the way he handled himself, made me feel like I knew the guy all my life. We were just two New Yorkers shooting the shit. Unconsciously, I reverted to the way we used to talk in the old Bronx neighborhood. "Go screw yourself" just slipped out.

Now seven years after that conversation, he calls me up to co-write his book.

Is this guy on the level?

After working twenty years on the FDNY, I had retired and moved to Florida. When the news broke on the morning of 9/11, I bolted immediately for New York, where I toiled at Ground Zero in the stench of rotting flesh, twisted steel, and crushed concrete.

When I returned to the Florida Keys, I systematically began sawing myself in half with bottles of Johnny Walker Black. After two years of drowning in whiskey, my mother's warning to me as a teenager resonated, "Always be wary of the drink, Billy. Alcohol doesn't run in our family—it gallops."

I had to get a grip on my genetic disorder and stop killing myself.

To turn my life around, simply turning to the next chapter wouldn't do.

So, at sixty-two years old, I put the plug in the jug and enrolled at the University of Florida. The professors in my journalism program taught me to write what I know, so I did. A weekly column I wrote went out to about 30,000 locals, called "Confessions of a Bronx Bookie." As an illegal bookmaker in New York for six years, I had frolicked in an underworld of felons, fixes, and phony finance, so I knew my stuff.

One week, I wrote a column about corruption in the NFL and a hypothetical Super Bowl fix. After rereading it, I brought it to my mentor, a top teacher in my school's program, and asked him to look it over.

"This is really good, Billy," he said. "I wouldn't give this away. I see it as a screenplay."

"A screenplay? Yeah, you know what? Maybe? But I've never written a screenplay."

"So what? I had Diablo Cody as a student a few years back. She had never written a screenplay until *Juno*. Look at her now. You're a writer. You can pull this off."

I took his advice and thought the screenplay that I wrote turned out pretty damn good. After graduation, I naively set out to L.A. to peddle it.

Matty, an old friend from the Bronx who had read a few of my columns, asked if I knew anybody out in Hollywood. When I told him no, he said, "Google Frank Pace. He was a trustee at Jacksonville University when I was coaching there. I think I can get you in to see him."

I Googled Frank's many accomplishments as a producer and what really gave me hope were his sports connections. I had a screenplay about a football game. He was Rod Carew's agent and a close friend of basketball legend Artis Gilmore.

I thought, wow, this story's right in this guy's wheelhouse. He might get it.

My appointment was at 11 a.m., so I arrived at L.A. Center Studios an hour early. No way I was gonna blow this. I had come too far.

After getting through two security checkpoints, I stood in front of the lobby's receptionist.

"My name is Billy O'Connor. I have an 11 o'clock appointment to see Mr. Pace." Her eyes dropped to a bound book in front of her. She nodded and pointed.

"The elevator is right around that corner. Mr. Pace is on the seventh floor."

I punched seven and reflected. I had to get through three checkpoints to see this guy. This was tougher than getting an audience with the Pope... six years of sobriety, four years of school, all leading up to this moment.

Now, my nerves were on edge.

I never had an ounce of fear lugging a charged hose down a smoky, snotty hallway to put out two or three rooms of fire, but shit, this was a one-time shot.

The elevator door opened to an outer office where a group of men and women pounded keyboards. The lady closest to the elevator said, "You must be Bill. Have a seat. Frank will be right with you."

True to her word, his door opened in a few minutes.

"You're Matty's buddy? Come on in."

Frank was about my age, weight, and size and wore tailored slacks with a blue Ban-Lon golf shirt. He shook my hand, retreated behind his desk, and pointed to a leather couch.

Once off my feet, I took a quick glance at the autographed pictures filling the frames on the wall. I recognized Don Rickles, Brooke Shields, Candice Bergen, Sandra Bullock, and George Lopez before I started to get it. Of course, I had never heard of Frank Pace. It's not his job to stand center stage. This guy works behind the scenes to make sure that the stars he works with shine.

Frank rested on his elbows, leaned forward, and spit out the sentence I had waited years to hear. "So, you're a friend of Matt's, and you've written a screenplay? Okay. Let's hear the pitch."

I quelled the bugs in my belly, took a deep lungful, and let him have it.

"It's about corruption in the NFL and a fixed Super Bowl," I began. "My yarn has two murders, loads of sex, and plenty of gambling."

I ran my mouth for five minutes, before leaping to my feet and excitedly running it for ten minutes more. I didn't even pause to grab a breath.

When I finally (mercifully?) stopped, I thought the poor guy's ears were going to start bleeding. I let out a sigh, smiled, and anxiously awaited his response.

An exasperated Frank let the left part of his lip bend into a small smile before saying, "Whatta ya have an air hose up your ass? Jeez, you didn't even stop to breathe."

He broke into a broad smile, shrugged his shoulders, and then poured vinegar all over my dream.

"I don't know, Bill. Who cares about a football game played decades ago?"

"Come on, Frank. Are you kidding? This story has got everything—the mob, corruption, gambling, and sex. Everything that made this country great." I grinned. "You don't think this is a cool story?"

"Not really," he said.

Then, with all the emotion of a guy bagging groceries, it slipped out. "Go screw yourself. This is a great story."

"Hold on," he said. "Did you just tell me to go screw myself?"

"Yeah," shoulders shrugging, the corners of my mouth turning slightly upward, "Yeah, I guess I did."

"I've got maybe a hundred people working with me on this lot. You come into my office on a friend's flyer looking for a favor, and you tell me to go screw myself?"

Oh boy, I really blew this one. What a schmuck I gotta be.

Frank said nothing and lifted the phone.

That's it. I'm getting the gate.

"Steve, get up here. I've got a crazy New York fireman in my office. This Irish lunatic just told me to 'go screw myself.'"

A few minutes later, Steve Wollenberg whipped open Frank's office door and lunged in. Dressed in a black muscle T-shirt, muscles upon muscle, his body seemed as wide as a beer truck. He had the bearing of a paid assassin. I might as well have been looking at Luca Brasi. Intimidating? That would be an understatement.

Steve exchanged a quick pleasantry with Frank, before whirling, striding three steps, and towering above the leather couch where I sat slack-jawed.

Steve's eyes narrowed.

"Are you the twerp who told Frank to go screw himself?"

"Yeah." Wide-eyed now, I whispered, "I guess I am."

Steve extended a hand as big as a catcher's mitt and broke into a wide grin. "You and I are gonna get along great."

The relief on my face had Frank grabbing his stomach.

Good God. These two pricks set me up. This guy Pace loves to break balls as much as I do.

Realizing what just went down, I burst into an orgasmic fit of laughter. After I had been cawing like a magpie for thirty seconds, they thought I was having a seizure.

When the gasping finally stopped, I tried to explain.

"You guys have to excuse me," I wheezed. "I have this ridiculous laugh. Once it starts, I can't catch my breath. I'm really sorry. People tell me that it's either contagious or annoying."

Frank leaned back in his chair and couldn't wait to spit out his next sentence. "Well, Billy, make sure you let us know when it starts to become contagious."

That crack earned him another dose of the magpie's mating call.

Frank and Steve showed me around the set of *Shake It Up*. Then the three of us went to lunch at the commissary. I let it slip that I had served a year in Vietnam. Steve was in Nam too. He was the real thing, one of those guys in the jungle, Steve would just say he was just doing his job, but in reality, he and all those there with him in that hellhole of Southeast Asia were heroes. We are so thankful for his service and the service of our many other brothers, 58,200 of whom didn't come back.

I went on to tell them that after Nam, I had worked humping furniture and appliances for the Teamsters before heading down to New Orleans to tend bar. When I came back to New York, I opened a couple of bars of my own and, to curb my misguided insatiable gambling habit, became a bookie. Then I finally hit the jackpot and got on the FDNY for twenty of the proudest years of my life.

It's still remarkable to me now. Just hearing Frank's voice had told me all I needed to know about what he was, who he was, and where he had come from. My instincts had taken over and made me realize that Pace wasn't immaculately delivered from the ass of a dove. He was just like me.

Within a couple of days, Frank had read my screenplay and gave me some invaluable advice. Over the years, we've stayed in touch only by emails and texts, yet he's read both my books and has always been more than kind with advice and encouragement. He told me that my first novel, *Confessions of a Bronx Bookie*, had dialogue so sharp you could shave with it. From a guy in his position, encouragement like that acted like a tonic.

After you've written a couple of books, friends call, congratulate you, and start pitching stories about their lives. Everyone thinks their lives will be a bestseller. When Frank called to ask if I wanted to collaborate with him, it was different. The stakes were higher. He had firsthand stories about household names, which he hadn't even shared with his mother. Now was the time for him to put them on paper.

He'd send me a chapter. I'd tighten it up, add a little color, and send it back. Then he'd do the same. We'd ping-pong pieces back and forth until we were both satisfied. The results were a fascinating read.

Frank often says he has a talent for remembering unique voices. Once he hears one, he rarely severs the connection. Well, we had only spoken in person once, seven years earlier, yet he asked me to work with him on *If These Lips Could Talk*. I just hope my voice, unique or not, can lend a hand in stringing some of Frank's stories together. With this book, I'm gonna do my best to switch places with him and act as his "ultimate sidekick." As the gambler in me would say, "From here on out, I'm all in."

IF THESE LIPS COULD TALK

"I'M IN A NEW YORK STATE OF MIND."

— *Billy Joel*

Chapter 1

MURPHY BROWN REDUX

When my flight out of L.A. finally mustered enough thrust to lift its undercarriage from the tarmac, most of my fellow passengers sat around idly getting ready for the cross-country jaunt ahead. Not me. Something weighed heavily on my mind.

It was May 2019, and I was flying to New York for the final wrap of *Murphy Brown*, the iconic sitcom whose return to television had begun with so much promise only fifteen months earlier. When the aircraft kissed the clouds and leveled off, my forehead rested against the small oval window, and I couldn't help but drift back to where *Murphy* had all begun three decades earlier.

In the spring of '88, Steve Papazian, the vice president of Warner Brothers Studios, had called and asked me to meet with show creator/ writer Diane English and her husband Joel Shukovsky to possibly produce their new pilot, *Murphy Brown*.

At the time, I was working as the producer for the third season of ABC's *Head of the Class*, but that wasn't a problem because pilots are shot while existing shows are on hiatus. Pilots were virgin territory for me, but with Steve's studio support, I felt confident.

Right out of the gate, I knew Diane English was special.

"Let's just make the best pilot we can," she said. "We'll worry about scheduling conflicts later."

So, we did.

We didn't make a good pilot.

We made a great pilot.

The show was immediately picked up as a series and put on CBS's 1988 fall schedule. That first season, we were nominated for six Emmys.

Murphy Brown won four but lost Best Show to *Cheers*.

Diane won Best Writing in a Comedy Series, which was remarkable because the pilot script was written before the writer's strike of '88. The strike ensured her first draft couldn't be revised or rewritten.

Imagine that? Diane's first draft had won the goddamn writing Emmy. So much for all writing is rewriting. That myth-exploding precedent was just a taste of things to come. Over ten seasons, *Murphy* would win eighteen out of sixty-two nominations and become a groundbreaker for female empowerment. It's on everyones list of the all-time great shows in television history.

The 1988 reviews for our new sitcom were practically rapturous. The *New York Times* wrote, "*Murphy Brown* is played with marvelously stylish élan by Candice Bergen. The sitcom doesn't get any better than this."

The Hollywood Reporter sang our praises even more colorfully: "Candice Bergen stars as *Murphy Brown*, hot-shot broadcast journalist and Betty Ford Clinic outpatient, who chews No. 2 soft pencils for lunch and goes through secretaries the way a rotary mower ingests swamp grass."

The critics were dead-on. Candice won five Emmys in the title role. She could have won more, but after her fifth win, Candice took her name out of consideration. She said Helen Hunt deserved to win for her role in *Mad About You*. When Helen did in fact win, she thanked Candice for her "generosity of spirit." Candice never again entered her name in the Best Actress category for *Murphy Brown*. All in all, our show produced 247 episodes of quality programing, including multiple wins for Best Comedy Series.

But that was then. This was now.

For years, Diane and Candice had been approached about bringing back *Murphy Brown*, but the incentive just wasn't there. They felt the show had said everything they wanted to say. In March 2017, the persistent Peter Roth, longtime president of Warner Bros. television, finally convinced Diane to write an updated script for *Murphy*. If Diane was game, so was Candice. Everyone agreed, however, if Diane wasn't happy with her script, no show.

By December, after putting writing off for months, Diane had completed the script and was indeed happy.

Peter showed the script to Les Moonves, the head of CBS Corporation, who months later would be "me too'd" out of his $60-million-a-year job. Les immediately ordered *Murphy Brown's* eleventh season.

Two caveats.

Diane only agreed to shoot thirteen episodes, and Candice would only shoot in New York. Peter said yes to both requests, so the band was back together. Murphy, Corky, Frank, Miles, and Jim were reunited. When I dropped Diane a congratulatory text, she replied, "Too bad we are shooting in NY."

After a quick consultation with my wife, I shot back. "Who said I won't go to NY?"

"Peter Roth's office will call you tomorrow," Diane texted back. She was delighted.

Just like that, *Murphy Brown* added a sixty-eight-year-old producer to join their brilliant seventy-year-old executive producer and their charismatic seventy-two-year-old star. Six of the original writers, also in their sixties, came back too. Instead of Warner Bros. studios in Burbank, the reunion would take place at Kaufman Astoria Studios in Queens. Other than that, it was old home week.

Subsequent months proved a blur of activity.

My job was to fly to New York, begin the staffing and oversee the designing, building, dressing, and lighting of the sets. Diane and the writers would toil in Burbank until mid-July. For the next two months at least, Diane's part of the deal would be easier than mine because I hit a huge snag.

Situation comedies and soap operas had migrated west years ago. New York had become a single-camera town.

Single camera means you shoot 360 degrees, one shot at a time. On a good day, you can shoot four to six pages of dialogue. We intended to reintroduce a multiple-camera format, shooting four cameras at once like a stage play. With this format, we can shoot forty-five pages in two days, meaning a lot of crew people who normally worked five days a week would have to commit to only two or three.

I needed every bit of my thirty years' experience, plus a few loyal staffers, to pull it off. I will spare you the gory details. Let's just say lots of blood was shed on stage that June and July. We turned over crew members the way Trump turns over his cabinet.

The New York way wasn't the L.A. way and vice versa, but we gave a little to get a little and ultimately got a lot. For the most part, I kept Diane out of the chaos. Some things of course she had to know, but I couldn't make my burden hers. She had to focus on the writing, which ended up the right call.

An elegant new newsroom was built, designed by Jane Musky. Renowned *Sex in the City* costume designer Patricia Field transported the cast's wardrobe into the twenty-first century. Every stick of lumber contained in Murphy's townhouse and Phil's bar had been meticulously recreated in Astoria. Everything looked the same, but things weren't really the same.

Twenty years had passed since *Murphy Brown* had last graced the airwaves. Diane was no longer married to Joel. Candice's husband, director Louis Malle, had passed, as had *Murphy* co-stars Pat Corley and Bobby Pastorelli. Gone, too, were Emmy Award-winning guest stars Colleen Dewhurst, Darren McGavin, and my dear pal, Jay Thomas.

Media demands for our revival were massive. Magazines and newspapers nationwide were sending their top writers to do feature stories. Morning, afternoon, and nighttime talk shows clamored for interviews. Everyone wanted a piece of *Murphy Brown*.

On July 21, 2018, everyone came to the stage to hear Diane's script. With expectations sky-high, the cast walked onto the stage charged with emotion, so much so that when Candice, Faith Ford, Joe Regalbuto, and Grant Shaud saw the sets, they broke into tears.

It shouldn't be too hard to understand why after nearly two decades, the cast members cried upon seeing the recreated sets. They had worked fifty-plus-hour weeks together for ten years—in many cases, more time than they had spent with their families.

To feed and clothe those families, they depended on each other to be at the top of their game, their product only as good as the weakest link. Nothing can be more American than working together for the common good. Stronger friendships and bonds were formed during those ten years than at any high school or college. Maybe even more than the military.

I'm never one to show emotion easily, yet at a certain time in one's life, the ebb and tide of waves breaking on a white, sandy beach or the setting of the sun are not insignificant events. I was at that time in my life.

Caught up in the emotion of the moment, a surge of satisfaction and gratitude coursed through my veins. After three long decades, Diane and Candice had remembered me and thought enough of my work to want me back.

Even the actors who weren't with the original cast were swept up in sentiment.

Tyne Daly had taken the place of the departed Pat Corley as proprietor of Phil's bar. We added Nik Dodani, a young stand-up who would become a breakout star, and Jake McDorman brilliantly played Avery, Murphy's twenty-eight-year-old, out-of-wedlock son. Avery's bastard birth had rocked America and Vice President Dan Quayle's sensibilities in a 1992 episode that drew 70 million viewers. Quayle was a straight-shooting family man who had translated the Old Testament into a political mindset that unfortunately seemed to preclude compassion—particularly when it came to matters of the flesh. Much like another Indiana native who will go nameless. (Cough, Mike Pence).

The table read was superb. We were off and running.

A comedy episode usually runs 21 minutes, 30 seconds. In 1988, the network had liked the pilot so much they gave us three additional minutes. This time Diane told CBS she needed six extra minutes. We told her she was crazy, but to our amazement, Diane being Diane coerced CBS out of the unprecedented six more minutes.

We shot the thirteen uninterrupted episodes like we were in a dream. Diane and her staff wrote the same brilliant material week after week while Candice and her cohorts played the roles they were born to play.

Some shows struggle to get guest stars, not *Murphy Brown*. Over the course of the new season, *Murphy* had Brooke Shields, Bette Midler, John Larroquette, Katie Couric, Andrea Mitchell, Peter Gallagher, Lawrence O'Donnell, and scores of Tony Award-winning Broadway stars.

Hillary Clinton even appeared on our first episode, which was fitting because Diane and Candice both agreed that if Hillary had beaten Trump, there never would have been a revival.

Hillary played one of the many applicants in our running gag of Murphy's never-ending quest for a secretary. Diane kept her appearance secret from everyone but the writers, a few of the suits in corporate, and me. Hillary first agreed to appear in July, but Diane insisted her guest spot remain hushed until the show premiered in September. Even the crew couldn't know.

That took some real cloak-and-dagger work.

We shot the episode in front of an audience without Hillary on August 1. Diane, director Pamela Fryman, and I had to figure out a way to seamlessly insert Hillary into the episode without anyone knowing it.

On the morning of Hillary's arrival, her aides and secret service needed access to the lot, so we clued in key people at the studio. Then we informed the makeup and hair people, so they wouldn't drop dead when Mrs. Clinton walked into their room.

Suffice to say everything went great. Mrs. Clinton was a delight. We had said no pictures, but more than graciously, Hillary posed for pictures with everyone who had a smartphone, which nowadays is everyone.

I expected to see the story break the following day on Page Six of the *New York Post's* gossip column, but to everyone's credit, the secret held until our premiere on September 27.

Now came the contracts.

I armed myself with two contracts, one for Hillary and one for my personal collection. Hillary's aides intercepted them and said her attorneys had to look them over first. To this day, they have never gotten back to us. Believe me, we tried numerous times.

Apparently, she had been told never to sign anything.

Murphy's cast was so unusually tight that after every show night, we retreated en masse to nearby George's restaurant. There the cast, crew, guest stars, stand-ins, and everyone connected to the show ate and drank to their hearts' content. Diane held court in a corner booth, clutching a celebratory martini, while Candice graced another table with her husband, real estate developer Marshall Rose; daughter Chloe; and her spouse, Graham. Candice loved sharing this new *Murphy* experience with Marsh. We treasured those Friday nights.

While some 9 million or so fans per week adored us, we were a very expensive show to produce, and truth be told, a lot of Americans just weren't buying a show with an unapologetic left-leaning agenda. Also, our 9 million fans put us squarely on "the bubble" for renewal with the network.

The high cost of producing a show in New York, exacerbated by a generation of twenty-somethings unable to watch *Murphy Brown* because it didn't appear on their streaming devices, burst our bubble. The new regime at CBS decided to chart their own path, and on May 13, Diane called with the sad news. We had been canceled.

Too bad. Reluctant as we might have been at first to take the plunge, everyone, especially Diane, Candice, and I, were all heartbroken.

So, here I was on a plane heading to New York. Tomorrow we would begin tearing down the stage. I felt like I did the day the wrecking ball tore into old Yankee Stadium, the end of an era. But what an era it was.

As Candice said, "We never would have gotten back together had the 2016 election gone differently, so if nothing else, I'll always be grateful to Donald Trump for that, anyway."

I agree with Candice. We should all be thankful for the remarkable circumstances that granted us that marvelous gift of a few more sunsets together.

(Postscript: When Karen and I returned from New York, we adopted a rescue puppy. We named her Murphy.)

Cast of the 2018 rebooted Murphy Brown with Diane English and Frank Pace. (PF Collection)

Secretary Clinton with the cast and crew of Murphy Brown. (PF Collection)

In the glory days! Pictured l-r: Candice, Diane English, Steve Papazian, and Frank. (PF Collection)

Publicity shot from the 1988 pilot of Murphy Brown with Candice and a Pope look alike. (PF Collection)

"TALENT IS LIKE THE PRETTY GIRL AT THE END OF THE BAR. SHE DOESN'T MEAN A THING IF YOU DON'T KNOW WHAT TO DO WITH HER."

– Brad Pitt

Chapter 2

FORTY YEARS WITH STALLONE, RAMBO, AND ROCKY

Yo....

Only one word, just two measly letters, yet they perfectly personify one of the most successful actors in Hollywood. One of the few stars in the business who can say with a straight face he didn't know a guy who knew a guy.

Now, he is the guy.

Forty-five years ago, Sylvester Stallone created Rocky Balboa, a seminal character of twentieth-century cinema. Stallone used his balls, hard work, and the sheer force of an uncompromised idea to climb the highest rungs of show business. He proved he wasn't just a one-hit wonder by creating yet another enduring hero, John Rambo.

Rocky convinced America that anything was possible. The movie was as simple as Rocky himself. With a budget of only $1.1 million and a production schedule of only twenty-eight days, Stallone transformed himself into an American icon.

Rocky won three Academy Awards.

Everything worked—the story, the characters, the casting, the photography, the turtles, the memorable music, everything.

A broke but courageously defiant Stallone refused $250,000 to walk away from his movie and let a bankable star play the lead. He was going to play the part of Rocky—or no one was. Hell of a move by anyone's standards.

Rocky II followed, as did *Rocky III*, *IV*, and *V*. On Christmas Day 2006, after a sixteen years hiatus, a sixth Rocky premiered. Ironically, this new film was called *Rocky Balboa*. Somebody decided that after thirty years of unimaginable success, Rocky needed his last name in the title. That, too, was a hit, followed nine years later by *Creed* and two more years later by *Creed II*.

Rocky II motivated me once and for all to make a career change to show business. Before entering that theater, I was a principal in a successful San Diego-based advertising and public relations firm, but I was tiring of the routine. Exiting that theater, I wanted to create the feelings in others the Stallone had awakened in me. I set off literally to reach for the stars. Ironically, my advertising background directly led me to my first of several encounters with Sly.

The first one came in 1981, when Lorimar Films hired our firm to consult on the movie *Victory*. The great John Huston was directing Sly, Michael Caine, and Pelé in a soccer-themed movie set during World War II.

My assignment culminated in a trip to D.C.

Stallone and Pelé were in the nation's capital to screen the movie for the press and appear at the North American Soccer League Championship Game. (That trip would later lead me to a dingy Los Angeles maximum-security jail and a meeting with the Hillside Strangler, but that's another story).

When we were introduced, Stallone extended his hand and said, "You're the guy handling the merchandising, right?"

This fella does his homework, I thought.

Impressed, I told him I had seen all four of his movies and even liked *Paradise Alley*, the movie that followed *Rocky*.

"Thanks, I appreciate that." His mouth twisted a bit. "But I watched that one with one eye closed."

We talked a little about *Victory*, and I commented about the bicycle kick, which Pelé used to score in the movie, "Pelé only scored five of those in his entire career." (A bicycle kick is extremely difficult and requires a tremendous amount of skill.)

At the next day's game, we hung out most of the afternoon in RFK Stadium's press box with Pelé, Henry Kissinger, D.C. Mayor Marion Barry, and a host of bureaucrats.

Stallone was scheduled to appear with Pelé on ABC for an interview at halftime. He had been assigned a second-row seat in the press box, but since Sly and I were the first ones in the room, I moved Mayor Barry's place card back a row, sitting Stallone right alongside Dr. Kissinger. With that simple maneuver, I had made a friend of Stallone for the rest of the trip.

At halftime, I took Stallone to the ABC booth, where we met Pelé. A clip from the movie was shown and included Pelé's bicycle kick goal. "Ya know," Stallone said, "out of the 1,300 goals Pelé scored in his career, only five came on bicycle kicks."

So, the guy does his homework *and* listens. That told me right then and there that he was the real deal.

I didn't see Stallone again for another year or so, but as I said, *Rocky II* helped inspire me to transition from advertiser to producer. I just wasn't quite doing it yet. I was still working for TPO in San Diego. One of our clients was New York based PONY sports and leisure, one of the top athletic shoe companies of the late '70s and early '80s. I never knew this at the time, but PONY stood for Property of New York.

Included in our stable of athletes were Wimbledon titleholder Tracy Austin, pro football's Earl Campbell, baseball's Reggie Jackson and Rod Carew, and heavyweight boxing champions Larry Holmes and Leon Spinks.

Spinks, during his brief reign as heavyweight champion, had been signed by Carl Ruhl, PONY's VP. Spinks's bodyguard at the time, Mr. T, would later sign to play Clubber Lang, Sly's antagonist in *Rocky III*.

PONY wanted Stallone to wear their boxing shoes for *Rocky IV*, so I became their go-between.

A meeting was arranged for my client Carl and me to meet with Stallone at Paramount Studios.

When we arrived on the lot, we were sent to a small building where Sly would be waiting for us. Expecting to see opulent offices, the building turned out to be Stallone's training facility.

There were weights, heavy bags, speed bags, dumbbells and a couple of boxing rings. Sly was sparring in the middle of one of them.

Sly and I exchanged amenities, and I introduced him to Carl Heinz Ruhl. My client immediately followed the handshake by interrogating Sly with his thick German accent. "I vant to ask you zumzing." Ruhl's eyes narrowed, his nicotine-stained teeth flashing a wicked grin through the thicket of a jet black goatee. "I haf known Mista T for three years, and zat muzzafuca couldn't zay his own name. How did you get him to remember all zoze lines in zat movie?"

Stallone paused, expressionless a moment. Then he shot Ruhl an even narrower look. "I paid him."

Stallone wore Nike in *Rocky IV.*

Mr. T would appear for me some years later in an episode of *Suddenly Susan*, playing cards in a scene with Donald Trump. Mr. T showed up wearing a four-piece dinner set around his neck: a plate, a knife, a fork, and a spoon. It was so funny, we let his silverware stay in the picture.

I worked on a film called *A Winner Never Quits,* which starred Keith Carradine as Pete Gray, a one-armed outfielder who played Major League Baseball for St. Louis during World War II. Ed O'Neill was also in the movie. Somehow during the filming, Stallone's name came up, and executive producer Dan Blatt asked me, "How did you let him get away?"

I didn't know what Blatt had meant at the time, but years later, I understood that the key to success in our business, any business really, is to cultivate and maintain relationships. Stallone had taken a liking to me, and I had let the opportunity pass.

Fortunately, my career took off, anyway, allowing me to work and maintain lifelong relationships with people I have written about in this book. Still, I had let Stallone get away. A show business lesson learned the hard way.

I'd occasionally run into Stallone in later years, mostly at Lakeside Golf Club, where he would spend his free time at the driving range. We'd trade a nod, a "yo," or a "how ya doin'?" and he'd continue banging balls.

Several years ago, we hooked up again backstage at a Don Rickles concert in Thousand Oaks. Rickles, a pal of mine, was always a must-see on every entertainer's list.

My pal George Lopez had never seen Rickles perform live, so we drove out to Don's show together. The crowd, including Sly, howled when Don introduced him as a "has-been."

After the show, Sly came up to George backstage and told him not to take any crap from anyone. "Keep doing what you're doing," Stallone said. "Remember, no one knows George Lopez better than you do."

Stallone asked me what I was doing these days, and I told him that I was producing George's TV series. Then he looked at me, looked at George, and gave George one last piece of advice.

"Remember this," Stallone said. "You're the star. If you touch it, you own it. Clothes, props, set dressing, light bulbs, whatever. If you touch it, it's yours."

At age seventy-two and with almost seventy movies to his credit, Stallone released *Rambo: Last Blood.* The movie trailer proclaimed, "you drew first blood, he will draw last."

This is one bad "muzzafuca."

Cue the music.

Sly and me. I had him and let him get away. (PF Collection)

Ed "Too Tall" Jones of the Dallas Cowboys and PONY Vice President, Carl Ruhl. (Courtesy of John O'Reilly)

MVP's Fred Lynn, Rod Carew, Reggie Jackson, and Don Baylor with their PONY shoes. (PF Collection)

"I WAS SUCH A DANGEROUS HITTER, I EVEN GOT INTENTIONAL WALKS IN BATTING PRACTICE."

— Casey Stengel

Chapter 3

ROD CAREW – SAFE AT HOME

"Watching Rod Carew bat is like watching Bulova make a watch, DeBeers cut a diamond. It is Baryshnikov dancing Tchaikovsky, Caruso sobbing out the clown aria, Kelly pirouetting in the rain. Rod Carew doesn't make hits, he composes them, the artist at bat."

— Jim Murray, Pulitzer Prize-winning author

My client Carl Ruhl called with the news.

"Reggie Jackson is coming to the Angels."

Ruhl had signed Jackson to a PONY contract in 1977, now he wanted me to be Reggie's West Coast point man.

"Go see him," he said. "Introduce yourself. Establish a relationship. Sign some Angels to PONY contracts"

So, on a crisp late March day in 1982, off I went to meet, in Reggie's own words, "the straw that stirs the drink."

With Angels batting practice in full swing, Reggie was what I expected, full of braggadocio. He looked me up and down and said, "You're a good-enough-looking white guy. Do you own a suit?"

"Yes, sir," I said.

"Do you own a tie?"

"Yes, sir," I repeated.

"Do you own a briefcase?"

Again, I said, "Yes."

"Good. Come back tomorrow. Put on your suit. Wear your tie and bring that briefcase—even if it's empty. We'll sign all these motherfuckers."

The following day, Reggie introduced me to several players, including Rod Carew, the seven-time batting champ. That friendship has had me representing Rod for almost forty years now. Our connection has made me realize that the tragedies and triumphs of Rod's life are not exclusive of each other, in fact they mutually coexist.

Rod was born on a train in Gatun, Panama, and was delivered by Dr. Rodney Cline, whom he was named after.

The abused child of a drunken father, Carew was often beaten and put in a dark broom closet for hours at a time. At fifteen, the rampant cruelty caused him and his mother to flee Panama and live with relatives in New York City.

Rod struggled with English but had no problem speaking balls and strikes, or so he thought. When he tried to make George Washington's High School baseball team, he was told he wasn't good enough, so instead he played sandlot under the shadow of Yankee Stadium at Macombs Field.

At Macombs, Rod was spotted by Twins scout Herb Stein, earning Rod a tryout inside "The House That Ruth Built." Twins manager Sam Mele watched the 150-pound Rod blast his first three pitches into the stadium's third deck.

Mele yelled to his coaches, "Get him the hell out of here before the Yankees see him."

Rod signed with the Twins on his graduation day and within twenty-four hours was shipped off to the Florida Instructional League. After a rocky start in the minors, he tried to quit the team several times—fleeing became a pattern of Rod's throughout much of his life.

Rod's Major League debut was in April 1967, in which he went two for five against the Orioles' Dave McNally. He knew then that he belonged. Under the watchful eyes of Twins' superstars Tony Oliva and Harmon Killebrew, Rod would play on his first of eighteen All-Star teams and go on to be named American League Rookie of the Year opposite National League pitcher, Tom Seaver.

He still holds the Major League All-Star record of fifteen consecutive years with the most fan votes at his position. Rod's 33 million total votes over the course of his career were more votes than Richard Nixon received in his victorious 1968 Presdential campaign.

When Billy Martin took over as manager of the Twins in 1969, Rod won the first of his seven batting titles. Under Billy's tutelage, Rod was encouraged to steal home. It became a habit. He swiped the plate seven times that season and sixteen times in his career.

Rod could have tied Cobb's record of eight thefts of home in '69. He still swears he was safe when the ump "guessed wrong" on a hairline play. He might have even stolen home an astonishing nine times had Harmon Killebrew not missed a steal sign. Carew was on third base and signaled Killer to let him know he was coming. Harmon was supposed to lay off the pitch and get out of the way. Rod gave the sign. When the pitcher when into his motion, Rod broke for home.

Killebrew hit a scorching line drive foul down the third baseline, missing Rod's head by inches. The next day, a Twins' beat writer suggested the following epitaph: "Here lies Rod Carew, lined to left by Killebrew."

Rod always felt "hitterish," and often joked that his favorite song was the national anthem.

"Every day that they play it, I seem to get two or three hits."

Rod never gave away at bats and often set up a pitcher by fouling off pitches that he could have hit, hoping that the pitcher would throw that same pitch in a critical situation later in the game or season. Rod was a greedy hitter who was never satisfied—when he got two hits, he wanted three. If he got three, he wanted four.

A student of hitting, Rod was difficult to strike out. He waved his bat like a magic wand spraying baseballs across the entire playing field. Angels manager Dick Williams once said that Carew had twenty different stances, and it was like pitching to five different guys.

The Twins won the division in '69 and '70 but fell short of the World Series when they lost to Baltimore's juggernaut teams. The mercurial Billy Martin left after the '70 season, but the lessons Carew learned from his mentor stayed with him throughout his career.

When Rod married a white Jewish woman in 1970, he would learn another hard lesson, one about interracial, interfaith marriage in America. Their three children would be born into a life of prejudice, prejudgment, and death threats. In addition to the racial intolerance, Rod had to be on the road half of baseball's eight-month season, which hardly made for a seamless marriage.

On one of those road trips in 1977, the Twins blew into Yankee Stadium. Rod was having a career year, earning him the coveted cover of *Time* magazine. He would finish the year only a handful of hits shy of Ted Williams's magical mark of 400, set way back in 1942. In the first of a three-game set, Rod added a couple of more hits to his already impressive résumé, really pissing off the reigning American League MVP, Yankee captain and catcher Thurman Munson.

The following night during batting practice, Munson, who would tragically die piloting his small private aircraft two seasons later, ambled past Carew and spit, "No hits for you tonight, big boy."

Rod just flashed a coy, competitive smirk. He knew that night's pitcher, Catfish Hunter, had chalked up twenty-plus wins for five consecutive years, but historically Carew ate Catfish like an overweight picnicker at a Carolina deep fry. He owned the former Cy Young Award winner.

In the top of the first, Rod came to bat and dug in from the left side. Squatting behind the plate, the gruff Munson reached in, threw dirt on Rod's shoe, and unlaced it. Carew knew Munson was trying to get inside his head and decided to do a little surveying of his own. He casually stepped out of the box, retied his shoe, turned to Munson, and flashed a smile as white as a nun's habit.

"Just for that, I am going to call every pitch that Catfish throws as it leaves his hand."

Munson looked up at Carew and sneered. "Bullshit."

Home plate umpire Ron Luciano suppressed a smile. It was on.

As Hunter wound up and released the pitch, Rod said, "Fastball down and in."

Sure enough, a fastball down and in.

Munson snarled, "You're peeking."

(When a batter peeks, he looks to see where the catcher sets up, so he knows the location of the pitch. An unwritten rule in baseball says no one peeks).

Carew took offense at the comment and shot Munson a sardonic smirk. "Throw the ball back to the pitcher, and I'll do it again."

Hunter delivered the second pitch. A fraction after its release, Carew called, "Slider, in."

Sure enough, it was a slider inside.

Fuming now, Munson called time and hustled out to the mound. By this time Luciano was smiling from ear to ear.

A defiant Thurman came back and said through his thick Fu Manchu moustache, "Catfish is going to drill your ass."

"No, he won't," Carew said. "Catfish has too much class to play those games. But just for that crack, I'll not only call the next pitch. I'll tell you what I am going to do with it."

As soon as the ball left Hunter's hand, Rod said, "Fastball away, double down the left field line."

Catfish delivered the fastball down and away, and sure enough, Rod laced a double down the leftfield line. As he was dusting himself off, Rod looked back to home plate umpire Luciano, who had both hands extended toward heaven and was bowing at the waist in an "I'm not worthy" gesture.

Thurman Munson never untied Rod Carew's shoelaces again.

Rod was voted the American League's Most Valuable Player in 1977, hitting .388 with 15 home runs and 100 RBI, the last RBI coming on the final at bat in the final inning of the final game of the season.

With Sam Perlozzo on second, manager Gene Mauch came out of the dugout to coach third base. He called time and jogged out to second base to speak to the rookie Perlozzo. With Rod's last bat of the season, the two-out message was clear: if Rod puts the ball in play, don't stop running until you reach the dugout. Rod made contact, and Sam took off like a wounded dog. When Mauch waved him in, bingo! RBI number 100.

A contentious breakup with Twins owner Calvin Griffith after the '78 season precipitated Rod being traded to the Angels. Carew was unhappy with some of Griffith's remarks and equated the flesh swap to a slave and his master. Things got nasty.

Some time later, Griffith claimed he had been determined to reward Rod for his marvelous career with the Twins, claiming he only traded him because he couldn't afford to pay him fair market value. Calvin and Rod reconciled years later. In January 1991, Griffith was the first person whom Rod called when he was elected in to the Baseball Hall of Fame.

The years must have made Rod realize that Griffith did him a favor. The Angels signed him to a five-year deal at $800,000 per, which was a boatload of money in '79 and a far cry from the $7,500 that Minnesota had paid him in his rookie year in '67.

In '79, the Angels won the AL West, but even with Rod hitting an extraordinary .412 in the playoff series, they again fell short of the Fall Classic, again losing to the Orioles.

In the 70s, Rod hit at an astonishing .344 clip. That spree continued into the new decade. Rod would spearhead the best hitting team I have ever seen. From top to bottom of their lineup, the 1982 Angels were loaded. The lineup had four former MVPs—Carew, Reggie, Don Baylor, and Fred Lynn—and thanks in large part to my buddy Reggie, all four players wore PONY shoes.

Sure enough, against the Brewers at home, the Angels jumped out to a two-game lead. Reggie hit a tape measure home run to deep center in the third inning of Game Two to extend the Angels' lead. Anaheim Stadium went crazy.

All they had to do now was win one of the three games back in Milwaukee to win the five-game series and punch their ticket to the Fall Classic. I was so confident that I had PONY World Series T-shirts printed with the Angels logo on them for all our guys.

It was not to be.

With two out in the ninth and the tying run on second base, Rod lined a ball into Robin Yount's glove for the third out of the final game, ending his last chance to play in a World Series. The Angels had lost three straight. Those T-shirts are somewhere on a playground in Panama.

Rod opened the following season at a.500 clip going a sizzling 48 for 96, but the Angels struggled and finished with a 70-92 record. Although continuing to excel at the plate, Rod's .338 average couldn't top young Wade Boggs for the batting title. Boston's marvelous hitter would eventually win four more.

Rod was injured early in the 1985 season, but at the Angels' request, he continued to play. His average dropped to somewhere near the Mendoza Line (.200). Several of us urged him to get an opinion from an independent doctor, one who wasn't on the Angels' payroll. When he did, it turned out that he had played the first two months of that season on an undiagnosed broken foot.

He went on the disabled list, returned in mid-June, and hit nearly.340 the remainder of the season. On August 6, against Twins' Cy Young winner Frank Viola, Rod became the sixteenth major leaguer to stroke 3,000 hits and joined Roberto Clemente as the second Latino to do so. That same day Tom Seaver, coincidently, won his 300th game. His contract expiring, Rod was told by Angels manager Gene Mauch that they wanted him back for his twentieth season.

A contract never came from the Angels or anyone else for that matter. With Major League rosters having been reduced from twenty-five to twenty-four players that spring, it seemed like something sinister was afoot.

Some late interest came from Al Rosen, the general manager of the Giants, yet the 1986 season was already underway. Rather than start over in a new league and a new city, Rod retired in early June. In his retirement speech, a defiant Carew said, "Baseball has been good to me, but I have been good for baseball too."

He knew he could have played at least two more years and was deliberately denied his twentieth season and longtime goal of making a goodbye trip around the league. In 1986, the Angels won the division again but didn't make the World Series. Rod's replacement, Wally Joiner, missed the entire playoff series because of a spider bite.

One can only imagine what might have happened if Rod Carew had backed up Wally Joyner that season. If the Angels, Twins, or any other team would have asked, Rod would have played for half his salary. No one asked. Rod put on a good front, but the snub by baseball hurt him. It was as if he was again the young boy back in that Panamanian broom closet. He took it personally, and has never really gotten over it.

One consolation came in 1988.

The courts awarded Carew nearly $1 million in damages when he was recognized as the first victim of owner collusion, dating back to 1986 The jury found that his release and forced retirement was the direct result of that year's calculated and deliberate effort of collective ownership to reduce team payrolls. He could have and should have played those two extra seasons.

Reggie Jackson always says if you're not voted into the Hall of Fame on the first ballot, you are not a true Hall of Famer. Rod was voted in on the first ballot with close to 91% of the votes, only the twenty-second player in history to do it.

His psyche partially restored by the Hall's recognition, Rod rejoined the Angels as a full-time hitting instructor in '92. In April the team made their first road trip of the season. After a night game against the Yankees, the team's bus driver fell asleep on the way to their next series in Baltimore.

Angels Manager Buck Rogers was severely injured in the crash and never managed a team again. Rod suffered neck and jaw injuries necessitating major dental reconstruction surgery—wounds sustained, ironically, by a man hesitant to take a coaching job because of his fear of flying.

In 1995, things began looking up for the Angels.

By August, they were heading to another Western Division title with a thirteen-game lead over Seattle. Then the Angels hit a losing skid. Seattle got hot, and everything went to shit. Even if it's your livelihood, in the grand scheme of things, baseball is just a game.

Life isn't.

That September, the Carew's would face every parent's nightmare.

Rod's youngest daughter, Michelle, his pride and joy, his beloved "Pish," was diagnosed with leukemia.

She asked the oncologist, "Do I have a chance?"

"A slim one," he said.

"That's all I can ask," "Pish" said.

Rod confided in me that he would have to do something. The intensely private and reclusive Carew did a 180-degree turn. In an effort to find a marrow donor for Michelle, he drew on his fame to become the public face of Worldwide Marrow Donors, swelling their rolls from fewer than 5,000 donors to nearly 70,000 within the year.

Ever moody, Rod became more and more morose when not around Michelle. He would often take long, solitary drives, sometimes as far away as Utah, then just turn around and come home. Often, we could not reach him for days. No one could. We were concerned but never despondent, knowing that Michelle had a bigger fight on her hands and Rod would never desert her.

Michelle succumbed to leukemia in April 1996. Gallant to the end, she never cried or felt sorry for herself. Before she passed, she whispered, "Daddy, if I die, don't forget the others. Work just as hard to save them as you did to save me." Rod learned a lot about courage from Michelle and promised to honor her request until the day he drew his last dying breath.

Although a broken man, he delivered an eloquent eulogy at Michelle's funeral on a rainy Minnesota day. When we left the church and entered the cemetery, the rain magically stopped, and a brilliant rainbow flooded the heavens. Michelle had lit up every room she had ever graced with her presence, so it was fitting that on the day of her funeral, she even lit up the sky.

Rod threw himself full bore into his vow and did everything humanly possible to keep Michelle's memory alive and to ensure those not named Carew be treated with the same care and dignity Michelle was.

He hosted the first Rod Carew Pediatric Cancer Research Foundation Golf Tournament that fall. Now in its twenty-fourth season, it has generated more than $20 million in Michelle Carew's name.

The next year, on a road trip to Baltimore in September, Rod had been invited by then-Senator, now-Governor Mike DeWine of Ohio to address a joint committee of Congress in Washington, D.C. Rod made a highly emotional plea to increase funding for childhood cancers.

Some weeks later, while Rod was on one of his long solitary drives, I called with great news. On his fifty-first birthday, the Congressional committee had appropriated $50 million to the National Institute of Health to study pediatric cancers. He pulled over. The tears painting his face said what his lips couldn't. He told me he just pointed to the sky at his beloved Pish.

A child's death either destroys a marriage or makes it stronger. In the case of the Carew's, their union became collateral damage. Rod and his wife separated and ultimately divorced. Although Carew had rightfully pushed baseball to a backburner, just to aggravate matters, the Angels let go of their entire staff.

One small shaft of light creaked through that avalanche of misery. As soon as he became available, the Milwaukee Brewers and I negotiated a deal for Rod to join manager Davey Lopes's staff and become the highest-paid hitting coach in the majors. When in-fighting broke out among some of the coaches and Lopes in Rod's second season, that flame died too. The Brewers were going nowhere fast, so Rod left the staff after the 2001 season and would never coach full-time again.

During Rod's brief time with the Brewers, he met and fell in love with Southern California native Rhonda Jones. When they married in December the following year, Rod adopted Rhonda's two beautiful children, which gave him a purpose other than baseball.

I suggested that he stay on the sidelines the following year since he was enjoying his new life. He had mellowed considerably since Michelle's passing and was becoming more receptive to new ideas. Rod was tired, anyway. He said he'd give it a try.

That August, Rod and I flew on Commissioner Bud Selig's private jet to Cooperstown for Tony Gwynn's and Cal Ripken's induction. Sensing I would never again have such a captive audience, I laid out a plan to Selig for Rod to return to Major League Baseball.

Selig said that he would get back to me. True to his word, several months later, Sandy Alderson, then the commissioner's number two man, and I worked out a deal. Rod became special advisor to the commissioner for international player development.

Now that the first phase of my plan was in place, the next step was to reestablish a connection with the Twins, an affiliation that had suffered immeasurably in the wake of that nasty collusion trial in '86. With the Angels, I feared our relationship was broken beyond repair.

The key to the Twins was their young president, Dave St. Peter. A regional native, Dave understood and valued the great history of the Twins and jumped at the idea of Rod's involvement. In 2003, Carew joined the Twins as special assistant to the president. He would attend spring training with the club every season thereafter.

That same year we made an exclusive agreement with MAB Celebrity Services to do four to five autograph shows a year, a commitment Rod still maintains to this day.

Then lo and behold, we caught another break when Arte Moreno became the new owner of the Angels.

With the Twins willing to share Rod, the then Angels VP of Media Relations (and now Hall of Fame President) Tim Mead and I hammered out a contract. Rod would rejoin the Angels in a part-time capacity.

Rod was safe at home again, finally.

At last, Rod seemingly had it all, a beautiful wife and family and great friends. He was working as much as he wanted, with people whom he loved, and doing what he wanted to do. Then life kicked him square in the ass again.

Rod went to play golf on September 20, 2015, and suffered a massive heart attack. The only bright spot was that it happened on the first tee. If he were playing alone somewhere out on the golf course, it would have been both his last round and last breath. He flatlined twice in the ambulance and again in the ER.

When I got to the hospital that morning, for all intents and purposes, Rod was a corpse. Rhonda and I were told his heart had failed. Rod would have to go on a Left Ventricular Assist Devise (LVAD) until his heart was strong enough to have a transplant.

No one outside of the family knew.

I contacted my old friend, Armen Keteyian, who was now working for CBS News, to talk strategy. We agreed to keep it quiet and wouldn't break the news nationally until Rod was out of danger.

We decided that Minnesota native Steve Rushin of *Sports Illustrated* was the logical choice. We dialed Steve, a magnificent writer who had grown up a Carew fan, and he instantly signed on. You can read Steve's story at: https://www.si.com/mlb/2015/11/23/rod-carew-heart-angels-twins

After reading Rod's story, former All-Star Angels pitcher Clyde Wright was motivated to get checked out too. Turns out, he had a 95 percent blockage and had to immediately undergo a five-way bypass.

Guided by their experience with Michelle's tragedy and in concert with the American Heart Association, Rod and Rhonda announced the formation of the Heart of 29 campaign for heart awareness.

At a Minnesota Twins Fest in late January 2016, the Heart of 29 campaign was unveiled. With a battery operated LVAD beating where his heart formerly had, it was Rod's first public appearance since the operation. Similar events soon followed at games played by the Twins, Dodgers, Angels, and Red Sox. Even the Baseball Hall of Fame hosted a heart screening for their members on induction weekend, and the Carew's couldn't have been more gratified to see the throngs of esteemed players and families attending to get heart checkups.

Honoring Rod that July, Major League Baseball announced that henceforth the winner of the American League batting title would receive the Rod Carew Award. His good friend, the late Tony Gwynn, would receive a similar honor. From that year on, the National League's batting award would bear Gwynn's name.

All was right with the world until August when more grim news struck. Rod was hospitalized in San Diego with a subdural hematoma.

The LVAD medication can cause bleeding, and it did in Rod. He had developed a clot on the brain, and the life-threatening condition made him delusional. He had been in the Marine reserves during his early years in Minnesota and begged me to round up his old buddies to help bust him out. Rod was forced to miss the PCRF tournament for the first time, so Rhonda appeared in his place and promised Rod would be back in 2017. A promise they were able to keep.

By October, Rod was better, but the clock was ticking. At seventy-one years of age, Rod was told by the surgeons that his kidney had been compromised by the stress of the heart attack, so he would need a kidney transplant as well as a heart.

In late afternoon of December 14, 2016, Cedars-Sinai called with a heart and kidney match. Rod was apprehensive, but Michelle had shown him what courage looked like years before. While the orderlies were wheeling him in for his transplant at 11 p.m., I stopped the gurney, placed my mouth next to his ear, and whispered, "It's the bottom of the ninth, score tied with two outs, and Catfish Hunter is on the mound."

Rod managed a weak smile and said, "I got this, then."

Rhonda and I spent a sleepless night in his hospital room. We put on a good face, but we were concerned.

A successful thirteen-hour operation ensued, and Rod's heart surgeon said he had transplanted a strong twenty-nine-year-old heart into Rod's body. Rhonda and I looked wide-eyed at each other. Was it only coincidence that the founder of the Heart of 29 received a twenty-nine-year-old heart?

The next day, Rhonda heard rumblings that the donor may have been a former NFL football player named Konrad Reuland, who had lived locally and died on December 12 of a brain aneurysm. Rhonda and I huddled in the Cedars commissary to discuss what all this might mean.

Heart recipients are not even allowed to ask the hospital who their donors might be for a full year, and then the donors have the right to reject the requests and remain anonymous. Rod was only one day post-op, yet Konrad's name had already surfaced. One thing Rhonda and I agreed on: under no circumstances would she call the Reulands.

Rod got past the critical thirty-day rejection period without incident and was released. During that phase, Rhonda had come home periodically to check the mail and get them both clean clothes. One day while checking her phone, there was a message from Mary Reuland, Konrad's mom.

Mary Reuland was relatively certain that Rod had received her son's heart but waited two weeks before calling the hospital.

"Was the recipient of my son's heart Rod Carew?"

The hospital staff was dumbfounded. The rules against recipients asking for the donor's name were clear, but they had never encountered a donor's family asking who the recipient was. They gave Mary their one-word answer: "Yes."

The Reulands, Doctor Ralf and Mary, and one of Konrad's two brothers, Austin, finally met the Carew's on March 2. Mary said that Konrad had met Rod at his son's basketball practice some eighteen years earlier. She remembered how excited Konrad was when he came home and told them he had met Rod Carew. Konrad even boasted to his two brothers that he was going to be a professional athlete.

Because no two heartbeats are the same, Dr. Reuland handed Mary a stethoscope and asked if she could hear her son's heartbeat. Having memorized Konrad's heartbeat, Mary burst into tears. Everyone in the room quickly followed suit, and a new family was born, the Careulands.

If you want to share in this remarkable scene, go to: https://www.youtube.com/watch?v=zbAawUji5jM

Was it a coincidence or fate that brought these two families together? I'd like to believe the words of an old adage, "There's no such thing as coincidence; coincidence is just God's way of acting anonymously."

Nothing will ever compensate the Reulands for the loss of their son. Nor will it compensate Rod for the loss of his dear Michelle, but such is the cycle of life that "the Lord giveth and the Lord taketh away." The Reulands and the Carews have since been blessed with new grandchildren.

The Twins, the Angels, and Major League Baseball are all happy that Rod's back to work, and Rod couldn't be more pleased that the heart from Konrad's 6'7" body fills his 6' frame.

In Rod's own words, "It races like a Maserati."

The cocky kid in Carew is still around too. Just the other day, a reporter asked Rod what he would hit if he were playing today. Rod paused for a moment, smiled, and said, "Probably about .280."

"Just .280?"

Rod had set the reporter up as he had set up so many pitchers years before, and like the pitchers, the reporter took the bait.

His smile broadened. "Hey, what do you expect? I'm seventy-four years old with a transplanted heart."

Rod was still feeling hitterish!

"Mr. October" Reggie Jackson, Frank and Rod Carew at the Field of Dreams in Iowa. (Courtesy of MAB Celebrity Services)

The Cooperstown shrine is forever. Here Rod is pictured with fellow Hall of Famers Bob Feller (l), Stan "The Man" Musial (r), and Tom Seaver (standing). (Courtesy of The Baseball Hall of Fame)

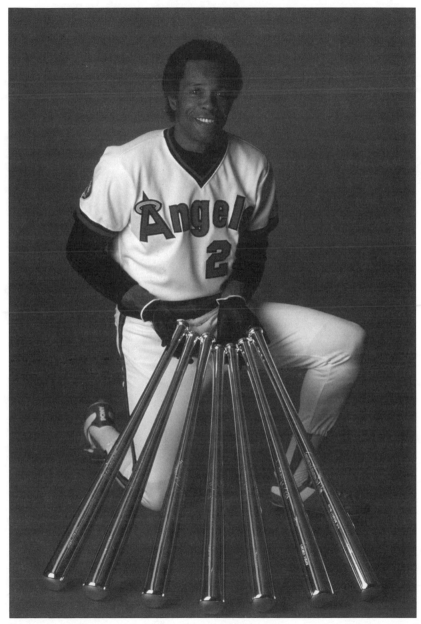

Rod with his seven Silver Bats, emblematic of his seven AL batting titles. Rod batted .344 for the decade of the 1970s. (Courtesy of Rod Carew)

"IF YOU DON'T HAVE ANYTHING NICE TO SAY ABOUT SOMEBODY, COME OVER HERE AND SIT NEXT TO ME."

– Dorothy Parker

Chapter 4

THE POLLY O MOZZARELLAS

The Official Book of Italian Street Slang describes a Polly O Mozzarella as: "Not the real wet cheese you purchase in delis, but a poor dry imitation wrapped in plastic that grocery chains push on people who don't know any better."

It goes on to say, "Polly O Mozzarellas can be a term used to describe phonies or pretenders, people who have neither original singular voices nor the foresight to stay true to themselves."

Sadly, I'm fairly certain that no *Official Book of Italian Street Slang* exists, but that doesn't mean I haven't run into my fair share of people who fit this definition of phonies. Many of these Polly O's might not even remember my name, but I sure as hell remember theirs.

However, one actress wrapped neatly in plastic who attempts to sell herself to people who don't know any better definitely knows my name. Kathy Griffin worked with me on the set of *Suddenly Susan,* a show I produced for NBC for four seasons.

One of several equally talented co-stars to Brooke Shields, Kathy always craved stardom. As the show went into its second and third season, Kathy got bolder and bolder in pursuit of her aspiration, demanding that the writers give her more Griffin-centric stories.

Of course, she never let Brooke, or her other co-stars, know what she was up to. Around them, she was all kindness and light. Behind their backs, she was spiteful and shady. In Kathy's mind everything was secondary to finding new material to advance her career and stand-up act.

The whiny temperament that her character Vicki Groener personified on camera played off stage as well. When we got to our fourth and final season, half the original cast was gone and replaced by new actors, including Eric Idle and Sherri Shepherd. As one of the survivors, Kathy felt even more bulletproof. The squeaky wheel got greased with even more screen time by an adoring new writing staff. If only they had known.

After our cancellation, Kathy starred in a successful reality show, *My Life on The D List*. She even won a couple of Emmys for her efforts. Kathy had found her niche, the D list, indeed, supplemented by a sweet little New Year's Eve gig with Anderson Cooper on CNN.

She was rolling.

The notoriety bolstered her stand-up act. Everyone whom she had ever had a beef with became cannon fodder. At the end of the show, being of no further use to Kathy and fueled by the breakup of Brooke's marriage to tennis star Andre Agassi, Shields became the target of some tasteless, exceptionally bitter barbs.

I spoke to Brooke years later on the set of *Murphy Brown* about those unwarranted and malicious remarks. She felt hurt and used by Kathy and still does to this day.

Hoping to capitalize on the anti-Trump sentiment sweeping the country, Kathy posed with blood dripping from the neck of the decapitated president. Her joke backfired and backfired badly.

As with most egomaniacs, she was self-destructing. Comedy venues around the country canceled scheduled appearances. Now box office poison, Griffin became a pariah and even lost her gig on CNN.

She made matters worse when she lambasted CNN's Jeff Zucker, calling him a pussy for caving into Donald Trump and then lamenting the lack of support from her former "dear friend" Anderson Cooper.

Ironically, when Trump had guest-starred on an episode of *Suddenly Susan* several years earlier, Kathy had kissed The Donald's ass as hard as it has ever been kissed.

Many years later, I had the misfortune of seeing her again at a funeral.

Against my better judgment, I went over to say hello. That was my mistake. She was ready for me.

"Hello, Kathy" I said, extending my hand.

"I'm sorry," she said. "Do I know you?"

Well it had been fifteen years, and who looks the same after fifteen years? I gave her the benefit of the doubt. "Frank Pace."

I didn't expect her to gush, but I expected that at least I would get a polite "Oh, Frank, how are you?" Instead, I got crickets and a blank stare.

"I'm sorry," she answered. "I still don't know who you are."

Screw me, I fell for it.

"You know"—my eyes hardened through a forced smile—"I produced *Suddenly Susan* for four years, and if I learned one thing in those four years, it's that you aren't a good enough actress to pull a charade like this off."

We haven't spoken since.

The nicest thing I can say about Kathy is I really liked her mom and dad.

I have often been asked who was my favorite person to work with?

That is a difficult question, as there are so many to pick from. Now ask me who was my least favorite and that is easy—former L.A. Dodgers manager Tommy Lasorda. He is not the jovial, overstuffed, happy-go-lucky persona he plays when the TV cameras roll. At 92 Tommy is living proof of the adage that only the good die young. Let me tell you a few quick stories.

We were scheduled to shoot a Chicago Brothers Pizza commercial with Tommy in L.A. one summer day. Noted television director Howard Storm was at the helm. Howard was big time, having launched both Robin Williams and Jim Carrey's careers. He was also a bantamweight fighter back in his Henry Street days in the bowels of New York City. I would call Howard a Jimmy Cagney type.

To say that he didn't take any shit from anyone was an understatement. Tommy had a 9 a.m. call, showed up at noon, and proclaimed he had to be gone by 2 pm, even though we had Tommy booked for the entire day. Howard fumed but held his cool. When it was time for him to get into makeup, Tommy said, "I don't need makeup."

The female costumer looked at Tommy's shirt, which he shouldn't have even been wearing in the first place, and politely asked to iron it. It was a hot morning, and Tommy had been riding and sweating in the car for ninety minutes. He was in desperate need of a new shirt, yet Tommy took umbrage at the mere suggestion.

"My wife ironed this goddamned shirt. If you think you can iron a damned shirt better than my wife, you have got another thing coming."

And so it began.

Tommy wasn't prepared, had not read the script, and didn't give a damn that he had been given an equity piece of the company to shoot this spot. After several starts and stops caused by Tommy's lack of preparation, I went over to him and introduced myself. He was gruff and impolite. Another nobody, he must have thought. (Well, he might have been right on that point).

San Diego Padres General Manager Jack McKeon, a client of ours at The Phillips Organisation and a friend, had warned me Tommy's behavior could be problematic.

"If Tommy gives you any trouble, tell him I said he was a traitor. He will know what I mean."

It must have been a code they had. If I was ever going to use that quote, now was the time.

"Jack McKeon says hello," I said.

"Right." Tommy said and turned his back to me.

He must have thought, no way this guy knows Trader Jack.

"He said to tell you that you are a traitor."

Lasorda spun 180 degrees, so did his attitude—toward me, anyway. He had been outed and knew I would report back to Jack about what an asshole he was. When we went back to shooting, however, Lasorda was no better than before. He was clearly not invested. Finally, Howard had had enough.

He went up to Lasorda and said, "Look, Tommy, can I tell you something? You *suck*! When this commercial runs, and it will most definitely run, nowhere will it say directed by Howard Storm."

Howard had fire in his eyes. Tommy backed down immediately.

After Lasorda made it through one take, Howard set up for a second.

"Why?" Tommy asked. "When my batter hits a home run, I don't wait for him at the plate and ask him to hit another."

"That is all well and good," Howard said. "But you barely hit a single."

With the use of some well-placed cue cards, we got through the day. Howard left without even shaking Lasorda's hand.

The second Tommy story occurs at the presentation of Don Rickles's star on the Hollywood Walk of Fame. Lasorda, my wife Karen, and I, along with twenty-four others, were invited by Rickles to a post-presentation luncheon.

We split into three pre-assigned tables of nine.

Tommy was put at our table with Elliott Weisman, Don's and Frank Sinatra's personal manager. Tony O, who was Don and Frank's road manager, was also at the table. Pretty good company, I'd venture.

Tommy pitched a fit. He went to Don and demanded to know why he wasn't sitting at Don's table. Don, gentleman that he was, moved his mother-in-law to our table and transferred Lasorda to his.

Don got his revenge. He roasted Tommy mercilessly in his thank you speech, even feigning tears over Lasorda's table assignment. Tommy cracked up. Knowing how sensitive Don was, it would have hurt him to accommodate Lasorda at the expense of Barbara's mom. This was his way of showing his displeasure.

That day, Tony O told me another story. It was well known in the inner circles that Tommy was a user. He was so tight you'd have trouble cramming a BB up his ass. He never paid for anything and Sinatra, a *huge* spender, was getting tired of it.

One night after a show, Lasorda bullied his way past the guards and made his way to Sinatra's dressing room, accompanied by a half dozen or so uninvited guests. He was going to play the big shot and introduce them to his pal, Frank. Frank accommodated Tommy, but as soon as they left, he turned to Tony O and said, "From this night on, he's dead to me," which in any dictionary, Italian or otherwise, means, "From this night on, he's dead to me." Tony O made sure Sinatra never spoke to or saw Lasorda again.

Tommy Lasorda sold out Billy Russell when his longtime shortstop replaced him as manager of the Dodgers. Lasorda even sold out his own son, Corky, a gay man, when he died of AIDS in the early '90s. To this day, Tommy never publicly acknowledges this truth. At the time of Corky's funeral, rather than asking for gifts to the AIDS foundation, Lasorda requested donations for retired baseball players down on their luck.

Imagine that?

But as bad as that was, instead of staying home to console his wife the night after his son died, Tommy took off to the ballpark where people could see him. Imagine not staying home to console your wife after her child dies?

Everything was always about Tommy.

To judge for yourself, listen to Lasorda's interview with well-intentioned reporters. Make sure you stay with it and listen how his venom builds as he gradually loses his temper:

https://www.youtube.com/watch?v=fzjWQF1oP2M

A comedy club in Pasadena was where I first saw another poser, Rosie O'Donnell. Although still an unknown, she tormented and reigned terror down on not only the staff but everyone around her. When we shot *Bless This House*, we cast Rosie as Andrew Dice Clay's little sister. You can see that, right?

Again, Rosie acted like a demon, driving the writers and Andrew to distraction with her script demands. Some days, she refused to appear on stage until Andrew was ready for rehearsal. It was painful to watch. Even Andrew had cause to pause. O'Donnell ultimately parlayed success in films, most notably *A League of Their Own*, into her own talk show, *The Rosie O'Donnell Show*.

The writers on that show told horror stories about their days on staff.

Suddenly Susan had shot an episode in which Brooke and Kathy Griffin's characters appeared with Rosie on her set. Her treatment of her staff and crew was inexcusable. As soon as that camera light came on, she turned as sweet as high fructose corn syrup. We couldn't sprint back to the stability of *Suddenly Susan's* stage fast enough.

Then came *The View*.

Rosie came to *The View* with a well-earned reputation as a difficult, demanding, and abrasive person. Take a miserable attitude, add problems with co-host Whoopi Goldberg, and then stir in behind-the-scenes battles with *The View's* upper management. It made for a calamitous cocktail.

A series of well-publicized battles with real estate mogul Donald Trump didn't help her cause. She left *The View* after a year, came back six years later, and then left again only nine months after that. Rosie made a brief return to the spotlight when her old adversary Donald Trump was elected president, but for Rosie, her race was pretty much run.

She too had been exposed.

My encounter with Todd Bunzl was another brief respite from the genuine article. Never heard of him? What about Todd Phillips... famed director of *The Hangover Trilogy, Back to School*, and a film that played to some rave reviews and made big bucks called *Joker*? Yep, the Academy Award-nominated director Todd Phillips. That's one Polly O who deserves a capital P.

In the spring of 2007, I received a call to interview for *The More Things Change*, an ABC pilot to be helmed by feature director Todd Phillips. Phillips had previously directed *Road Trip* and *Old School*, so this was a big deal for me. When I met with the co-executive producer, Scott Budnick, he glanced at my résumé and saw that I had produced pilots for *Murphy Brown* and *George Lopez*. He was impressed. Following my short interview with Phillips, Budnick hired me on the spot.

The cursory, one minute interview with Phillips was like sampling cold pizza or sipping a warm beer. It left a bad taste in my mouth. I was happy about being hired, of course, but something wasn't right.

In the production business, all production is pre-production. Planning ahead eliminates as much guesswork as possible. Producers try to anticipate all potential scenerios to prepare contingencies and have backup plans ready just in case. This way when the actors show up, the director can focus on getting their best performances. The director is vital, as he has the last word.

My concern was that Phillips had never directed a TV pilot. Don't get me wrong. I knew Phillips could do the work. The question was, would he?

In television, the creative process is accelerated. The size of your budget is understandably less. You can't throw cash at a problem. That was at the root of my concern.

Phillips stood to earn mid-six figures for this seven-day shoot. A feature film shoot usually lasts thirty to ninety days, occasionally more. For a director at Phillips's level, the financial rewards are obviously greater. Still, this gig was hardly a benefit. With the up-front director's salary, negotiated royalties for each time any episode aired for the life of the series, and potential back-end payoff, Phillips stood to rake in a nice stack of chips.

Despite the monetary incentive, other than casting, Phillips refused to prep. He met with the production designer only when absolutely necessary to go over the sets, and instead of scouting locations, he relied on video tape.

He even declined to tech scout. (Traditionally, after locations are picked, we visit each site with department heads to develop a strategy for the day we arrive. Every detail is discussed with the director—right down to where we will eat and where we will park the trucks).

Hell, Phillips didn't even appreciate why we had to do a table read, which is mandatory for network and studio notes. He then refused to read the stage directions, forcing us to hire someone to perform that task.

Phillips was obviously phoning it in to collect a paycheck. When the cast arrived, he was fine and obviously knew his stuff. However, when the camera wasn't rolling, Phillips, who would later date Paris Hilton, spent most of his time trying to hustle the female extras.

Morality aside, that type of unprofessional behavior just sticks in my craw.

He was ultimately savvy enough to hijack the terrific production designer I had hired, Bill Brzeski, for his future projects.

The very definition of a Polly O'Mozzarella, Phillips changed his last name and was intimately involved in the shady, high-stakes card game depicted in the feature film *Molly's Game*. He was also booted off *Borat* for what were considered "creative differences" with Sacha Baron Cohen. With Phillips gone, Cohen went on to be nominated for an Academy Award for his work. The film capped 2006 by being selected as one of the top three films of the year by many major publications, including *Time* magazine and *The Washington Post*.

After my experiences with him, I could see why Cohen had gotten rid of him. It was Phillips's way or the highway. Cohen showed him the highway.

When *The More Things Change* wrapped, we converged in the editing room.

"What are you doing here?" Phillips asked me.

"I am here for the editing."

In Todd Phillips's world of feature films, this is unheard of.

"Leave," said Phillips.

Refusing to blow my cool, my left eye narrowed.

"I have produced thirteen television pilots, and eleven were sold. How many pilots have you produced?"

After begrudgingly having to answer my question with "none," he agreed that I could stay. Despite knowing my input would be ignored, just to spite the arrogant son of a bitch, I stayed.

The More Things Change consequently got chalked up on the wrong side of my scoreboard. I had now produced fourteen pilots with eleven winners.

Too bad.

That promising script had "director neglect" stamped all over it. Phillips never gave a second thought to the cast, writers, or the 100-plus crew who had put their hearts, souls, and dreams into it. Many would end up unemployed the next season because of their commitment to that failed pilot.

Phillips would go on to direct all three *Hangover* movies, partner with Bradley Cooper to produce *A Star is Born*, and followed that up by producing and directing the mega-hit *Joker*. Not a bad résumé. His efforts have earned him well over a half a billion dollars.

By financial measures, Phillips could be the most accomplished comedy director of all time. Now reaping the monumental rewards from *Joker*, he has taken that success to another level. To this day, I refuse to see anything he has directed.

The last Polly O Mozzarella is Goose Gossage, the hard-throwing Hall of Fame right-handed reliever for several teams, most notably the New York Yankees. Now in fairness, I only met Goose one time, but I had a doozy of an experience with him. In the summer of 1985, I was writing a book with Rod Carew and Armen Keteyian called *Rod Carew's Art & Science of Hitting*.

By this time, I had moved to Los Angeles. Gossage was now a member of the San Diego Padres, a team that would win the National League pennant that season. I had many friends on that team from my years as a PONY shoe rep in San Diego. Two hours before game time was when writers usually had access to the dressing room. I wore Major League Baseball's requisite media-access pass around my neck and said hello to Tony Gwynn, Alan Wiggins, and a few other friends before spotting Goose seated next to another former Yankee, Graig Nettles.

They were talking, so I waited politely to approach. I probably was a bit too polite, thereby tipping my hand.

"What do you want?" Nettles asked dismissively.

"I'm writing a book with Rod Carew," I respectfully explained. "I'm starting every chapter with a pertinent quote. I was wondering if Goose could give me a quote that I could use for my chapter on relief pitchers?"

Goose had experienced some success against Rod as a closer, making Gossage a perfect choice. If Goose had said no, I would have thanked him for his time and moved on. But Goose didn't say no, not exactly, anyway.

He and Nettles looked at each other and giggled like schoolchildren. Gossage smirked snidely through his trademark fluffy Fu Manchu, which had intimidated so many hitters throughout the years, and said (and this is exactly what he said), "Yeah, sure. I'll tell you what. Give me about twenty minutes. You go down to the left field foul pole, take a seat, and wait for me there. I will come down and give you the quote."

Then he and Nettles looked at each other and shared what I would say was a conspiratorial giggle. I nodded, thanked them politely, left with my hat in hand, and thought *stronzos*. You can look that Italian word up for yourselves.

When the Angels returned for their next homestand, I told Rod what had happened. He didn't say a word. I thought he didn't hear me, so I let it be.

Cut to spring training 1992.

I had long since forgotten my exchange with the former Yankee, but Rod apparently had not. Gossage, just past his fortieth birthday, was fighting his age and hanging in for one more paycheck from the Oakland A's.

He approached Carew, now a hitting coach with the Angels, and wanted some information. Rod looked at him and said, "Yeah, sure. I tell you what. Why don't you go down by the left field foul pole, take a seat, and wait for me there. I will be right down to talk to you."

Eight years later, Rod had remembered the slight almost word for word and got his retribution.

That's my man.

It says a lot more about who Rod is than who Gossage was.

It also reinforced a good lesson for me, one I have repeated many times to young artists. Don't fuck with anyone you don't know, even if you think it can't possibly come back to bite you in the ass later.

I once produced a pilot for Carlos Mencia, a Honduran-born stand-up comic Polly O'ing himself off as a Mexican. The creator of the project was Marco Pennette, whose work includes *Desperate Housewives, Ugly Betty*, and, more recently, the hit series *Mom*.

In my interview with Marco, he said, "You don't remember me, do you?"

When I copped to the fact that I didn't, Marco said, "I have an aunt from Armonk, New York, who knows your mother from North White Plains."

His aunt had spoken to my mom, and in the way that all proud moms do, she had suggested to his aunt that when Marco ventured west, he should "look up her Frankie, who was a producer in L.A."

I heard this and blanched.

Uh oh. . . .

"I hope I was nice to you?" I warily joked.

"You were beyond nice." Marco laughed. "You spent almost an hour with me at a time when I needed the support. I'll never forget your kindness."

The plain of causality is clear. As certain as night follows day, what goes around comes around. The smallest of acorns could grow to be the mightiest of trees.

Marco's certainly had. So, be kind and stay authentic.

I will have the caprese salad, please, and make the mozzarella extra wet, none of that phony stuff for me.

Kathy Griffin, Donald Trump, David Strickland, and Nestor Carbonell in a scene from Suddenly Susan. (Courtesy of Getty Images)

"THE FIRST HUMAN BEING WHO HURLED AN INSULT INSTEAD OF A STONE WAS THE FATHER OF CIVILIZATION"

– Sigmund Freud

Chapter 5

DON RICKLES – MR. WARMTH

Rod Carew and I were in Atlantic City for a baseball card convention some years back. Don Rickles was also appearing there. I called Tony O and arranged for tickets.

At the end of his shows, Don introduces any celebrities in the crowd. That night was no different. "Ladies and gentlemen, we are honored to have a true American hero with us tonight. Winner of seven batting titles, a Most Valuable Player award, more than 3,000 hits, and a member of the Baseball Hall of Fame, Rod Carew." After the applause died: "And he is here with Frank Pace, who is a fag for the FBI."

"A fag for the FBI"? What does that even mean? Admit it, though, you laughed.

I learned how to work in this business and how to be a decent, caring human being from Don Rickles. Don and I worked on a short-lived TV show, *Daddy Dearest,* a comedy created by two terrific writers, Billy Van Zandt and Jane Milmore. Though the show only lasted thirteen episodes, Don still made it the best show I have ever worked on. *Daddy Dearest* featured Don Rickles as a character who, after his recent divorce from Renée Taylor, moves in with his son, Richard Lewis. Richard played a psychologist, and Rickles's character was, in Don's words, "a pain-in-the-ass old Jew."

I christened Don "The Babe Ruth of Comedy," and he was. His legion of worshipers in our biz was legendary, from President Ronald Reagan to Sinatra to Jerry Seinfeld. Al Michaels called Don the funniest man he had ever met on a broadcast of *Monday Night Football.*

Don's star power drew big celebrities to appear on our show: Angie Dickenson (the sexual obsession of every adolescent boy who grew up in the '60s), Adrienne Barbeau (the sexual obsession of every adolescent boy who grew up in the '70s), Alex Rocco (the sexual obsession of—nah), and Barney Martin, amongst others. When Alex Rocco showed up for our table read, he and Don had never met. Don asked everybody to welcome Moe Greene, Alex's character in the epic *The Godfather* movie. Then Don re-enacted the scene where Mo got shot in the eye, finishing by face-planting himself into a plate of scrambled eggs.

By far the biggest guest star we ever had was Frank Sinatra. This took some massive coordination between Don, Tony O, Elliott Wiseman, and me. Don asked Frank if he would appear on the show. Frank's answer, "Yeah, sure, kid, whatever."

A week would go by and Tony O or Elliott would ask Frank if he remembered telling Don he would do the show. Sinatra would say, "Sure," but Tony O had warned me that even though Frank had committed, that didn't mean he would show up. We had to pick a date.

Sinatra's schedule couldn't fit into our normal Monday through Friday workweek, so we had to keep the set up and shoot a sixth day.

We used a swing set for the scene shot in a Vegas casino.

Swing sets are erected for specific episodes, but they're temporary. An expensive proposition to accommodate a man whom we had been warned might not show up, no matter what the day.

We were told the earliest Frank would be at the Hollywood Center Stages would be 11 a.m. We gave the crew a 9 o'clock call. At 9:10 a.m., Tony O called.

My heart skipped.

"Frank's up," Tony said. "He remembers that he's supposed to do the show. Which is good, but we are not home yet. I will call you after he's had his eggs."

The phone rings again at 10:15 a.m.

"He's just out of the shower," Tony said. "And he's still coming."

"What is he wearing?" I asked.

"I don't know what in the hell he is wearing," said Tony O. "He is wearing what he wears. Just be glad he is still coming."

At 11:05 a.m., Tony calls again. "We are rolling. Be there in about thirty minutes."

Director Howard Storm rehearsed the scene, so each member of the camera crew was precise in their shot assignments. All Frank had to do was hit his mark and say his lines.

With that, everyone on the stage had one last bathroom break and did their final looks at wardrobe and makeup. They were ready. Frank was coming, but he wasn't staying long.

Don's son, Larry, was working for the show, so I sent him out to meet the car, figuring Frank would welcome a familiar face.

Sinatra arrived wearing dark slacks; a pale-colored, long-sleeved open neck shirt that highlighted his blue eyes; a slightly dated but still fashionable lightweight Members Only cobalt jacket; and custom-made black leather boots with a side zipper.

Elliot, Tony O, and especially me all breathed a sigh of relief. Sinatra was really going to happen.

Getting anxious, I turned to Rickles. "How was Frank's mood the last time you were with him?"

Rickles looked sincere. "Frank's fine except he's got Sicilian Alzheimer's."

"Sicilian Alzheimer's? What the hell is that?" I asked.

Rickles deadpanned, "He only remembers the grudges."

The bastard got me again.

We knew we might get only one chance at the shot. The moment Sinatra entered the stage, we started rolling.

Frank was shown his mark and bellowed, "Where's Rickles?"

Don dashed in from offstage.

"You're wearing a tie for this bit?" Frank asked.

"Frank, please," Don said. "Don't embarrass yourself. Just stand there. Do the line and hope someone remembers who the hell you are."

My heart dropped. We didn't need Sinatra walking off the set, but Don knew his audience well. Sinatra doubled over with laughter.

Frank did the line once, then, surprisingly, did it again, and even bitch-slapped Don to punctuate the second take. He said his goodbyes and was off. Total elapsed time on the set: 3 minutes, 56 seconds.

Now came the contracts. Frank was famous for not signing anything. As he was getting into his car, I quickly thrust two SAG contracts in front of him. He signed both on the top of the town car, got in, and left. Truth be told, SAG only requires one copy of any contract. I have the second framed in my house: Performer Frank Sinatra, Producer Frank Pace.

One night on *Daddy Dearest*, Richard Lewis felt like he was having a heart attack. We rushed him to the hospital. The doctors said it was just a panic attack, but they would have to keep Richard overnight. The problem was we had already admitted the audience. Don saved the night. He gave a classic Don Rickles impromptu set that gave everyone in the audience *more* than they had come for. Don lit up the studio that night.

Richard was a real beauty. If you can believe it, he's actually more neurotic than the character he played. Don, Barbara, Karen, and I all attended Jane Milmore's outdoor wedding. While Jane was walking down the aisle, Richard dropped to the grass and started doing pushups. My wife, Karen, often said she'd like to smack Richard's mother for screwing him up so much.

In 2005, Richard finally met and married the love of his life, Joyce. I couldn't be happier for him. In later life he has even found renewed acting success on HBO's current hit *Curb Your Enthusiasm*.

After each show, Don, Tony O, and I would retreat to Rickles's dressing room and polish off a bottle of vodka. His wife Barbara was usually there, but on select nights, she wasn't. Tony O would then break out Don's favorite, pigs in a blanket. Man, those were good times.

As the show progressed, we started adding more and more of Don's outtakes to each of the end credits. By the last episode, our end credits stretched to almost four minutes. If you want to see the definitive *Daddy Dearest* outtake reel, check it out on YouTube.

Don often said that for two men to truly be friends, their wives have to get along. Barbara and Karen hit it off famously. They could talk for hours, never even remotely addressing Don or me.

Don did a hilarious imitation of Barbara as a spoiled Beverly Hills housewife that always made Karen and me die laughing, while Barbara would just roll her eyes. It was great theater.

Barbara was his rock. Don depended on her for everything and would never take a gig without her being present. They would often jet home the last night of a tour to sleep in their own bed.

Karen and I went on the road with them, out for dinner, and often went to their beach house for a home-cooked meal. Heaven forbid they would ever come to Pasadena. Don made me laugh, but I cracked him up as well.

He would call my house and say, "Frank, this is Don."

"Don who?" or "What do you want!?" My feigned indifference cracked him up. Indifference? Nothing could be further from the truth.

We were also privileged to be invited to Don and Barbara's birthdays and anniversaries and even their daughter Mindy's wedding. Family and friends were everything to Don and Barbara.

In retrospect, the highlight of my professional career was Don's seventieth birthday party. It was an incredibly star-studded event, even for Hollywood. More than 300 people attended. I told Don how glad I was that he didn't have to cut two people from the invitation list because my wife and I would be the obvious victims.

The guests included Frank Sinatra, Robert DeNiro, Sharon Stone, Bob and Ginny Newhart, Milton Berle, Marty Scorsese, and Red Buttons, along with Hollywood moguls Marvin Davis and Bob Daly.

We sat with comic Jack Carter and his wife and noted cosmetics maven Tovah Borgnine (and wife of Academy Award winner Ernest), plus Lorna and Milton Berle. Dinner service was a little slow. When they served the bread, they skipped Milton's.

With that, Lorna leaned over and, without asking, snagged my dinner roll.

"Milton's is hungry. Do you mind?"

It was pretty funny.

Another night, Berle and Forrest Tucker both showed up at Chasin's restaurant. The place was abuzz. Legend has it that those two have the biggest dicks in Hollywood. Was this the night that America would finally get its answer? Milton asked his agent for advice.

"They want me to go into the men's room and see who has the bigger dick, Forrest or me," he said.

The agent dragged from his cigar, paused for a moment, and then casually said, "Just take out enough to win."

Milton definitely deserved that dinner roll!

Don roasted the entire audience the night of his birthday, especially Scorsese and De Niro, who had just shot *Casino* with him. DeNiro was there with his wife, a beautiful black woman. You can imagine the slings and arrows that couple had to endure.

At the end of the dinner, they brought out the cake. Sinatra was asked to lead the group in singing "Happy Birthday."

"I usually get ten Gs for doin' somethin' like dis," Sinatra said.

It was absolutely perfect. I joked to Karen "my career is all downhill from here."

Larry Rickles continued to work with me through the mid '90s. He was an exceptional writer who earned a spot on the writing staff for the tenth season of *Murphy Brown*. Larry then co-produced *Mr. Warmth: The Don Rickles Project* with director John Landis for which Don received a long-overdue Emmy. Larry also earned an Emmy as producer.

Once, we were sitting in Don's house looking at photos of him and other famous people. Don commented wistfully, "Frank—dead, Dean—dead, Sammy—dead. John Wayne and Johnny Carson—dead. Newhart—almost dead," he said of his best friend with a twinkle in his eye.

Little did Don know that soon afterward, his dear Larry would be gone too.

In 2011, Larry died of pneumonia at age forty-one. Who dies of pneumonia at forty-one? Don and Barbara spared no expense to keep him alive. They, along with the doctors at Cedars-Sinai hospital, waged an epic battle, but in the end, they couldn't save him. Don and Barbara were devastated. They went into seclusion for several months. Don put up a brave facade, but he would never be the same.

We still delighted in our dinners with Don and Barbara at Craig's in Beverly Hills, but Don was beginning to slow down.

The last time we saw Don was at The Rose nightclub in Pasadena, where he was appearing with Regis Philbin in November 2016. Don Rickles, the song and dance man, was now restricted to doing his act seated but, man, was he funny. He gave me a kiss after the show and said we would all get together after the holidays. That would never be. Don died the following April, and the world got a whole lot less funny. Don was fond of saying, "If you have your health and are surrounded by people who love you, that's all anyone has a right to ask."

Don was the only man I ever met who had no enemies. To a life well lived. You were the "Babe Ruth of Comedy," indeed.

At the funeral service, Barbara served pigs in a blanket.

L'chaim, my friend.

The Chairman of the Board with his long-time road manager, Tony O. (Courtesy of Tony O.)

Don always said for two men to be friends, their wives have to really get along. Karen (l) and Barbara got along famously. (Courtesy of Barbara Rickles)

Don, the only man I knew who had no enemies. (PF Collection)

STANDARD AFTRA ENGAGEMENT CONTRACT

Agreement Between

Dated: September 13, 193

FRANK SINATRA

and

Home Box Office, a division of
Time Warner Entertainment
Company, L.P.

(hereinafter called "Performer")

(hereinafter called "Producer")

Performer shall render artistic services in connection with the rehearsal and broadcast of the program(s) designated below and preparation in connection with the part or parts to be played:

TITLE OF PROGRAM: "Daddy Dearest" DD9307 "You Bet Your Life"

TYPE OF PROGRAM Sustaining ( ) Commercial ( ) Closed Circuit ( )

SPONSOR (if commercial):

NUMBER OF GUARANTEED DAYS OF EMPLOYMENT:
(if Par. 19 of the AFTRA Code is applicable)

PLACE OF PERFORMANCE* . Hollywood Center Studios

SCHEDULED FINAL PERFORMANCE DAY: . 9/13/93

AFTRA CLASSIFICATION: . Principal

PART(S) TO BE PLAYED: . Himself

COMPENSATION: . $458

MAXIMUM REHEARSAL HOURS INCLUDED IN ABOVE COMPENSATION:
(if Par. 56 (b) of the AFTRA Code is applicable)

Execution of this agreement signifies acceptance by Producer and Performer of all of the above terms and conditions and those on the reverse hereof and attached hereto, if any.

Performer

Producer

Frank Sinatra
Social Security Number

By:
Frank Pace
*Subject to change in accordance with AFTRA Code.

Frank Sinatra's performance contract framed and hung in my house. (Mitchell Haddad Photography)

"BEFORE YOU CRITICIZE SOMEONE, WALK A MILE IN THEIR SHOES. THAT WAY YOU'LL BE A MILE AWAY FROM THEM, AND YOU'LL HAVE THEIR SHOES."

– Billy Connolly

Chapter 6

GEORGE LOPEZ – AMERICA'S MEXICAN

I owe Sandra Bullock a favor. If not for America's Sweetheart, I would never have met George Lopez.

Sandy Bullock is no ordinary woman. No woman ever is, but anyone who has ever seen *Miss Congeniality, The Blind Side*, or, *Ocean's 8* has fallen in love with this larger-than-life movie star. Yet, as lovely as she is on screen, the movies don't do her justice. Besides being charming, beautiful and wonderfully complex, Sandra possesses an indefinable intangible. She has a remarkable eye for talent and what works on camera.

Bruce Helford wanted to meet Sandra Bullock, the movie star, not the person. Helford likes to say he was a student at Jacksonville University when Artis Gilmore was there. I like to say that too.

Bruce is a brilliant writing savant. I produced three of his creations. The first was *Bless This House*, starring Andrew Dice Clay and Cathy Moriarty of *Raging Bull* fame. Bruce had originally hired me to produce *Drew Carey*, but when he sold a second pilot for *Bless This House*, he pulled me off *Drew Carey*.

He told me I had to "handle Dice," who was a delight with me and the crew, but in the weeks to come, he would christen Bruce with the pejorative, "The Bug." Anyone who has ever seen Dice's act doesn't need me to elaborate on his penchant for breaking balls.

Dice had enough talent to carry the pilot and beyond. Here was a stand-up comic who had sold out Madison Square Garden two straight nights. I was all in.

The pilot for *Bless This House* was a huge hit. Bruce had given me one percentage point of the adjusted gross on the back-end. Back-end points are everything in Hollywood, so I felt like I was holding a straight flush. No one at Warner Bros. thought much of the *Drew Carey* pilot, so it looked like I had made the right choice.

Deborah Oppenheimer replaced me on *Drew Carey*, and she had been offered the same back-end deal. That was fine with me. I thought Drew was an asshole and his show didn't have much of a shot. I called Deb to hedge my bet just in case.

"You give me 1/2 of your point on *Drew Carey*. I'll give you 1/2 of my point on *Bless This House*." I proposed. "It's a win-win situation."

Deb didn't agree, so we never made the deal.

As luck would have it, the lettuce ate the rabbit.

Bless This House went off the air after fifteen episodes. *Drew Carey* went on to produce more than 200 episodes, making Deb's point worth millions.

On the heels of *Bless This House* was the second Bruce Helford-created show that I produced, called *Nikki*, which ran for forty-four episodes, a damn good run. Toward the end of *Nikki,* rumor had it that Sandra Bullock was stopping by the stage with Bruce to see how multi-camera shows were shot.

Sandy was an actress and producer out of the single-camera world who was looking to create a multiple-camera show. As I said earlier, Bruce just wanted to meet Sandra. He wasn't really interested in what Bullock was selling. Bruce, no fool, soon became interested. Sandy was selling George Lopez—the most electrifying stand-up comic I have ever seen in person.

George, as history shows, took America by storm. As usual with show business, a little luck is always involved. In order to get Sandra Bullock on board, ABC agreed to give the show a commitment for six episodes that spring or a guaranteed spot on the fall schedule.

Peter Roth, the President of Warner's TV, gathered Sandy Bullock, George Lopez, Bruce Helford, Robert Borden, Gesine Prado (president of Fortis Films), and me into a large conference room to get our opinions.

Peter, Sandy, George, and I clearly wanted to go on the air with spring episodes rather than risk the fierce fall competition.

Bruce and Robert were worn out after writing a full season of *Drew Carey*. The prospect of shooting six episodes of a new *George Lopez* was unappealing. The room was at an impasse. Without Bruce and Robert aboard, we couldn't take the spring option. Then I had a thought.

I grabbed a scrap of paper and speedily scribbled. I slipped Peter the note, which asked a hypothetical question: "Is it easier to get a show on the network schedule or to keep a show on the schedule?"

Peter answered as I knew he would. "I must remind everyone here that it is easier to *keep* a show on the air than it is to *get* a show on the air."

We compromised and shot four episodes.

Good thing we did.

We discovered while editing our first episode that George had a peculiar tic. His eyes would bug out every time he delivered a punch line. It was a disconcerting habit. If we had only done the pilot, we would not have stood a chance when the Lopez pilot was stacked up against our competition. We withheld the first two episodes from the network until episode three was completed. Then we hit them with all three. George, a quick study, was by then over the bug eyes, and by episode four, we were off to a six-season run.

Prior to George's first episode, as is standard on any show, the network, studio execs, and executive producers inspect the sets to give their opinions. Deb Oppenheimer, by now Bruce's "hatchet gal," spit out that the kitchen didn't look "Mexican enough." I could see George seethe.

Should we put some jalapeños around the door? Wait until you put the damn Mexicans in it. Then it will look Mexican."

The kitchen stayed as is.

Throughout our six seasons, Sandy was a working executive producer, a continued presence, and a steadying influence on both the show and George. She even acted in a few episodes.

George Lopez is clever and complex and can be one of the most generous people I have ever met, but George has another side. He demanded absolute trust, to the detriment of everyone around him and almost to the point of obsession. Very few people could meet his exacting standards. If you crossed him, you were screwed.

George and I bonded over golf and baseball. I was always respectful of George but told him what I thought. He appreciated that.

George was so into golf that we built a driving cage above the dressing rooms, so he could practice his game.

Early in our second season, a turning point in our relationship came during one of those rounds of golf. George told me that he thought he was being woefully underpaid and was going to demand an immediate raise.

"Or what?" I asked.

He never answered.

"Wait." I said. "Let the show get a little more established, then come back in season three and ask for a boatload of money."

He did just that and made more than he could have ever imagined.

George Lopez was a great show to work on but not to write for. George was one of the boys, and he was a real ballbuster. We had a prop man named James Ide.

"What are you, James, Japanese or Chinese?"

"Japanese, George." He sighed.

"Same ting," George would gleefully squeal.

On and on it went. One jab was more inappropriate than the other. Another time, we had two children on the show, so we used two little people as stand-ins.

They were standing next to our prop master when George shouted, "One and Two Half-Men!" a not-so-subtle reference to another Warner Bros. show.

George could take it too. He always believed that in order to make fun of other people, you must be able to make fun of yourself first.

As I mentioned, one year I had the opportunity to take George to see Don Rickles. As was his custom at show's end, Don introduced celebs in the crowd. When it came to George, Don said, "It is my great pleasure to introduce a big, big star, George Lopez. Never in my life did I ever think that I would be passed up by a damned Mexican."

George followed Stallone's aforementioned advice about touching everything and had a hand in every story. This is another reason it was such a tough show to write for.

"Hell, the writers can't do George Lopez without George Lopez," he often said. He gradually got more and more assertive. He even directed an episode just to prove to everyone that he could do that too.

During our second season, I pitched George an idea that I had for a story. After he approved, I brought it to Helford who green-lighted it. In the story, George had been invited by his best friend Ernie and his dad to attend the '78 baseball All-Star Game in San Diego.

My plot revolved around George catching a foul ball and getting four All-Stars to sign it. The ball becomes George's prize possession—a symbol of the dad he never had. The ball stands in a case alongside four Bobblehead dolls, representing the All-Stars who had signed the ball. George's son, Luis, swipes the ball to play with and destroys it.

I now had to come up with four players who had played in that game, which wasn't hard. Rod Carew hit two triples in that 1978 game, and I had known Steve Garvey for fifteen years. Rod's fellow Hall of Fame members Joe Morgan and Jim Palmer were easy adds, so we were in business.

The four Bobbleheads came to George in a dream and reminded him that his son was more important than any old signed baseball. George had a great time doing that episode, "The Unnatural," as did the pro ballplayers. I think that episode helped solidify my relationship with George, and I got my only "story by" credit to boot.

Toward the end of season two, the show was reaching its peak of popularity. George, now approaching forty-five years old, was finally a superstar. He was playing to sold-out arenas across the country, appearing in celebrity golf tournaments nationwide, and had even taken over as host of the Bob Hope Chrysler Desert Classic.

I suggested George write a book about his life. I had just the author in mind for him, too—my old pal Armen Keteyian. Armen and George hit it off, and during the third season of the show, *Why You Crying?* debuted on the *New York Times* Best Seller list.

But trouble was lurking.

It was about seventeen episodes through our twenty-two-episode run for the third season when George pulled me aside. He had a rare disease. Both kidneys were failing. In need of a transplant, he was racing the clock to get through the season. We had to keep it quiet.

"You know that dented tomato soup can that everyone avoids in the supermarket?" George said. "I don't want people in this industry looking at me like that dented can."

George's wife, Ann, would be the kidney donor. Only his manager and I knew about it. I also knew I had to protect George's secret, as every week his condition got more dire.

It got to the point that I would do the shooting schedule on the usual camera days, but our pre-shoot schedule often made no sense at all. Once, assistant director Rosario Roveto Jr., who is a smart guy, questioned my judgment. I bowed my neck, pointed my index finger, and told him, "When you know what I know, then you can have the corner office, not just a podium on the stage."

We made it through the season, and within a week of wrap, Ann gave George one of her kidneys. TV and weekly news programs covered the event, as did the newspapers *People* and *Us* magazines. They were America's heroes.

George and Ann divorced five years later.

While hosting the Bob Hope Chrysler Desert Classic, George got close with his boyhood idol, Lee Trevino. From here, George will tell the story as published in the October 12, 2007 issue of *Sports Illustrated*.

For me, as a kid, growing up in Los Angeles's San Fernando Valley, golf was invisible. Hell, I was invisible, if not disposable. I was a young Mexican American who didn't know his father and whose mother left him to be raised by a grandmother. In golf terms, I started life out of bounds with a three-putt and a snowman.

My first memory of golf was watching it on TV where I saw someone who not only looked like me, but someone who had grown up dirt-poor and been abandoned by his father too; yet he had gone on to become one of the greatest golfers of all time. Because of Lee Trevino, I was the first person in my family to wield a club that wasn't swung in anger. Trevino became my symbol of opportunity.

During the ensuing years, I turned my opportunity into professional success, which eventually allowed me to become friends with Trevino. One September, I lured Lee back to Pebble Beach for the first time in 22 years to be my professional partner in the Wal-Mart First-Tee Senior-Champions tour event.

Lee and I had scheduled a practice round the day before the event. He wanted to go to Cypress Point, one of the most exclusive courses in the world, but I had already booked us a tee time at Pebble. Luckily, I persuaded him to come over, or we would have missed one of the proudest moments of both of our lives.

As we strolled toward the green on Pebble's 3rd hole, a downhill par 4, the sight of us two Mexican golfers with white caddies caught the attention of the maintenance staff. I guess the fact that it was Lee and I had something to do with that as well.

All work stopped and many of the laborers gathered to watch us play through. I realized that in a way, Lee and I were walking symbols of opportunity for these men who were working so hard to prepare the course and to create a better life for their families.

The superintendent approached and asked if we wouldn't mind getting in a photo with his guys. I noticed a large lawn mower nearby and asked to have it brought over. Then I called to Lee, and we all climbed aboard.

You'll notice in the photo that the driver's seat is empty. That's to symbolize that we are all equal and that anyone, regardless of race, gender or financial status, can rise to captain the ship and control his or her fate. Lee did, I did, and so will some of those men.

It's my favorite shot of all time, and the photo hangs proudly in both Lee's house and my own. Perhaps it's appropriate that it was taken with a disposable camera.

I also played in that group and was there to take the photo. In our tournament round the next day, I got off to a rough start. We had a gallery of about 700 following us around the famed Pebble Beach links. After I hit my fourth wayward drive into the rough, Lee ambled over to me and chuckled. "Relax, Frankie, no one is here to see you."

My life story in a nutshell. Boy, was he ever right. I was with them, the perennial sidekick.

In 2008, George and I produced a special for the Golf Channel entitled *Lopez and Trevino*. We went to Lee's home in Dallas to shoot parts of it. Our old pal Jim Huber narrated. That special was a cut above, and I'm more than proud of it.

During our sixth season, my friend Perry Rogers invited George Lopez and me to a lavish fundraiser in Las Vegas for the Andre Agassi Preparatory Academy. Andre and Perry had spent the day prior to the event showing both of us around this magnificent school.

Andre had built the academy from brick one. Although located in one of the worst parts of Las Vegas, this rough ghetto took so much community pride in Andre's school that not a lick of graffiti stained the outside walls and the interior was as clean as an operating room.

The school caters to the less-fortunate children in Las Vegas, grades K through 12. The entrance requirements are rigid. Each class is limited to twenty per grade, so capacity is roughly 260 needy kids. Once the students graduate, and roughly 99 percent do, Andre has forged relationships with a network of colleges to help them advance.

If a potential student has any financial means whatsoever, they needn't apply. Everything is out in the open, lockers, computers, everything. Kids wear uniforms and adhere to a strict set of rules. Meals are included, which is a big attraction. If one rule is broken, no matter how minor or inconsequential, the student is expelled. One strike and you are out at Agassi Prep.

No one even thinks about breaking these rules.

All students' expenses are borne by Andre and the Foundation. Each year, the school runs a black-tie fundraiser in the ballroom of the MGM Grand, an area as large as Madison Square Garden and the site of such notable prize fights as Mayweather versus Pacquaio. It is the same arena where Mike Tyson gobbled off a chunk off Evander Holyfield's ear in their epic second fight.

Although the MGM Grand is a large space to fill, those guests who pay a healthy sponsorship fee to attend receive an opulent dinner followed by a live auction.

After the live auction, the doors open, and the public swarms in. Each pays a healthy fee to fill the remaining 18,000 seats of the dual levels of the great ballroom to see a list of talent that, over the years, have included Elton John, Barbara Streisand, Stevie Wonder, Robin Williams, Eric Clapton, Michael Bublé, and Celine Dion. Services for the entire night, including the entertainers, are underwritten or donated—100 percent of everything will go to the school.

George, our wives, and I were seated alongside Andre, his new wife Steffi Graf, Robin, and his wife. George and I were clearly feeling good about ourselves. Andre had collected some wild prizes to be auctioned live, including all-expenses paid round trips to *all four* grand slam tennis events.

That's a first-class vacation to Sidney, London, New York, and Paris, or if you prefer not to travel, how about a private dinner for ten in your home prepared by Chef Emeril Lagasse?

You get it, right? Really big stuff.

So, now, time came to auction off a private concert by the group

Earth, Wind & Fire. You know their tunes: "Reasons," "Shining Star," and "September."

George turned to me and said, "Wouldn't it be great if we could get Earth, Wind & Fire for the wrap party of our show? How much can we afford?"

Not wanting to look like a tightwad in front of all these high rollers, I whispered, "Maybe $25 grand."

"I will match you out of my pocket," George said. "So, we will be good for $50 grand."

George started the bidding proudly at $20,000. We came out swinging to scare off the little fish. No sooner did the sentence hit the air, than another voice yelled, "$25,000."

George went to $30,000 and again a voice yelled, "$35,000." George's stride shortened a bit now. Shit, we were thinking we can't go bust in Vegas over something like this.

George shouted, "$40,000."

The auctioneer asked, "Do I have $45,000?"

Someone else shouted, "$45,000."

This is our last chance, but it wasn't looking good. We looked at one another, and George blurted, "$50,000."

Two other bidders wanted it besides us. If the bidding went beyond $50,000, we were cooked. We were straining our necks to see whom we were bidding against, but the room was so massive and the lights so bright we couldn't make out the other bidders.

Good thing we couldn't see. The bidding volleyed all the way to $250,000 with the winning bid coming from none other than Vegas hotel tycoon and multi-billionaire Steve Wynn.

With these guys bidding, our fifty large bought barely enough grease to stop the cookies from sticking. Who could've figured we'd crap out against real high rollers? Hey, what were the odds?

After a six-year run, we thought we were getting picked up for another season, but ABC canceled the show. They opted instead to pick up a show that they owned 100 percent rather than a seventh season of a show that they owned none of.

The show was *Cavemen*. How did that work out? George went ballistic and said some things that he was right in thinking but probably not right in saying. That is why America loves George. He say's what he thinks, and he thinks what he says. Right or wrong, he speaks his mind.

George Lopez was just a launching pad. George has gone on to host his own network talk shows, star in feature films, and continue to sell out with his stand-up. He still finds time to guest star for an old friend when called upon.

So, thanks, Sandra. I do owe you one. George is truly America's Mexican.

George's favorite photo, with Lee Trevino and the greens crew at Pebble Beach. (Courtesy of George Lopez)

With Sandra Bullock and sister, Chef Gesine Prado, at the world premiere of Ocean's 8 in New York City. I owe you one, Sandy! (PF Collection)

Hollywood Wise Guys. Clowning on a set with George Lopez and director Joe Regalbuto of Murphy Brown acting fame. (Courtesy of George Lopez)

"THE ONLY MYSTERY IN LIFE IS WHY THE KAMIKAZE PILOTS WORE HELMETS"

– Al McGuire

Chapter 7

THE DICEMAN/POETIC JUSTICE

"Where's 'The Bug'?" Dice bellowed. "Bring me the damn 'Bug.'"

Andrew "Dice" Clay was screaming on the set of *Bless This House*, demanding the presence of the show's creator, Bruce Helford.

Bruce, the story savant who created *Bless This House*, would never be mistaken for a runway model. He is 5'6," 100-and-nothing pounds, and wears his hair in a sort of reverse Mohawk, which fittingly enough is the name of his company, Mohawk Productions.

His bald head perched atop his scrawny neck was accentuated by an unappealing growth of hair under his lip. The "bop" seemed a carefully cultivated accessory added to make his features appear worse. Yet make no mistake. This uninviting vestibule only served as camouflage for the brilliant intellect inside.

When I showed Bruce's picture to my co-author, Billy O'Connor, he said, "Good God. Whatta mug. I bet he doesn't get laid much."

"Trust me," I said. "With his money, he gets laid anytime he wants."

Dice of course is Andrew Clay, the talented costar of *A Star Is Born* who in the late '80s was also the biggest stand-up comic in the country. The Diceman and Bruce were paired together in the winter of '95 when Helford created *Bless This House*. Bruce cast Dice as the show's lead, Burt Clayton, a blue-collar mailman struggling in Trenton, New Jersey, with his wife and two kids.

Burt's neighbor was his best friend and co-worker. The two men's wives were also best friends. Sound a bit familiar? It should. It was basically *The Honeymooners*.

Andrew Silverstein had cut his teeth doing stand-up comedy. His alter-ego, Andrew Dice Clay, had leapt to prominence as a chain smoking, black-clad, motorcycle-jacket-wearing, limerick-spouting persona whose foulmouthed act tapped into a racist, homophobic, mostly white male audience.

No one was safe. He offended everybody equally, even the "little people" whom he called "midgets!" Who could ever forget these poetic classics from Dice's act, "Little Miss Muffet sat on a tuffet eating her curds and whey, along came a spider and sat down beside her and said, 'Hey, what's in the bowl, bitch?'" Or this one, "Mary, Mary, quite contrary, trim that pussy, it's so damned hairy." Or "Jack and Jill went up the hill, each with a buck and a quarter. Jill came down with $2.50... that whore!"

As his audience got older and the world got more politically correct, Andrew's star cooled. His bent for self-destruction didn't help either. In 1989, his three-minute set of the above dirty nursery rhymes earned him a lifetime ban from MTV.

Despite that, only months later, Dice had become the first comedian to sell out New York City's Madison Square Garden on consecutive nights.

Yet within a year of that unprecedented achievement, Nora Dunn and Sinead O'Connor refused to work with Dice on *Saturday Night Live*. Controversy plagued his career, leading to a quasi-meltdown on the *Arsenio Hall Show*. Dice broke character that night and left the stage near tears.

Bless This House would be his comeback vehicle. By this time, he was just Andrew Clay. Ironically, it would be a comeback of sorts for Bruce Helford too.

Bruce had risen through the writer ranks to become executive producer on *Roseanne*. Roseanne Barr hated him and fired him before the year was out. Roseanne was wrong.

When Bruce and I discovered that we had concurrently attended Jacksonville University, he said, "I can't believe you didn't attend any of my plays."

"How many of my soccer games did you go to?" I countered.

In an unusual deal, one which I had never heard of before and haven't heard of since, Bruce's writing contract was "traded" from Disney Studios to Warner Bros. for future considerations.

That wasn't the only thing unusual about Helford. He was also superstitious and eccentric.

Bruce wouldn't fly, ever. It's not the flying Bruce was concerned about. It was the time between the flying and the dying. He believed the color red was jinxed, forbidding even the use of red script covers. He also insisted on never using the term "show" in a series title, thus *Roseanne, Drew Carey,* and *George Lopez* were named exactly that.

At Warner's he created two series simultaneously, *Bless This House* and *Drew Carey.*

The *Bless This House* pilot script was excellent, as was the casting of Bronx-born Cathy Moriarty of *Raging Bull* fame as Alice Clayton. (Notice the similarity—Alice Clayton, Alice Kramden).

The first day of the pilot, Cathy was near the craft service table, and I wanted to introduce her to our dialogue coach, Marty Nedboy. I never did a show without my good luck charm, Marty, another self-described "old New York Jew."

I called to Marty, "Come here. I want you to meet somebody."

He glanced in our direction and yelled from across the stage, "I already met Shirley."

Marty had confused the Academy Award-nominated Moriarty with our craft service lady. Cathy just laughed. She, too, would come to love the funny, eccentric Nedboy.

Everything went great on the pilot right up until the Friday afternoon shoot. Cathy showed up "overmedicated" from cold medicine and passed out in the makeup chair.

We blocked Cathy's scenes with a stand-in, but when it came time to pre-shoot a couple of more scenes, Cathy was still out of it. I had to invent a technical problem with two of the four cameras, which would make the pre-shoot scenes impossible.

Chuck Reilly, our technical director, was sworn to secrecy. No one could know. Cathy sort of snapped out of it in time to get through the evening show, but Andrew heroically stepped up and really carried the night.

The show was sold to CBS, and we were on the air. When the show debuted in the fall, we got several good reviews, a first for Andrew.

One New York paper wrote, "It really does remind you of *Jackie Gleason and The Honeymooners* without trying to copy that classic. There could be life after for Dice; this kinder, gentler Andrew Clay seems like a pretty decent guy." The *Los Angeles Times* also gave it a favorable notice, writing, "*Bless This House* doesn't quite blow you away, but it's a pleasant half-hour with likable characters and enough start-up humor to make you optimistic about its future."

In a surprise to almost everyone, *Drew Carey* also sold. I am told that the execs at Warner Bros. TV were so down on the show that they didn't even want to take it to New York for the advertising upfronts. They finally acquiesced and were pleasantly surprised by the outcome.

That's when the problems started.

As good as he was, Bruce couldn't be everywhere at once.

We moved into two offices in the same Building 140 on the Warner's lot. *Drew Carey* would be on the first floor, *Bless This House* the second. Not a confrontational person to begin with and perhaps burned by his experience on *Roseanne*, Bruce moved into a first floor office. That was the first of many slights perceived by Dice.

To aggravate matters, Bruce turned the writing chores over to my old friends Billy Van Zandt and Jane Milmore. Two terrifically talented writers but not the ones Andrew had signed up for. Don't get me wrong. Andrew really liked Billy and Jane, but they were running the show in name only. Bruce was the boss, albeit from afar.

Bruce would drop into the *Bless* writing room at 10 p.m. and change almost everything the staff had written. He also was going through a separation, so the running joke was that both shows were working every night till 3 a.m. because Helford had nowhere else to go.

As the show progressed, we saw less and less of Bruce. Andrew became empowered and reverted back to being Dice again. Now, "Where's 'The Bug'?" became Andrew's common refrain to emphasize that he knew damn well that Bruce was missing from the stage.

The more Andrew acted out, the more Bruce avoided him, giving Andrew the opportunity to start slipping his Dice-isms into *Bless This House*. Little things like his signature unlit cigarette reappeared hanging from his mouth or his insistence on getting the phrase "It's a touchy situation" into every script.

Still, the show was rolling on at Christmas break. CBS execs asked Cathy Moriarty to host the network's coverage of the Rose Parade from Pasadena. Cathy had been a delight, despite her bump in the road on the pilot. We thought we had it made, until Andrew, who had self-destructed the first time he approached superstardom, did it again.

CBS was happy enough with our ratings, but we were taking a beating in the press. The more conservative outlets, remembering

Andrew from his Diceman days, wanted him banished from network television.

Les Moonves had been president of Warner Bros. throughout the shooting of our pilot. Then he got a big job as president of CBS. He was firmly invested in *Bless This House* as long as things were going well. Over the two-to-three-week holiday break, the emboldened Andrew demanded a meeting with Les.

I am told that in the meeting, Dice laid out his unhappiness with Bruce. He insisted Helford be taken off the show. Les told Andrew he would get back to him. The Rose Parade came and went as it does every New Year's Day. Cathy as usual was great in her Bronx kind of way.

The following Monday brought a lot of enthusiasm to stage for our fourteenth show's first day of rehearsal. After the table read, the writers, the director, and I met with the network and the studio executives as is customary to get their notes on the script. The phone in the green room rang. Bruce answered. It was Les. For the first time in his life, Helford was speechless.

Moonves had been given the out he needed, not that he really needed one, and he canceled the show. Our fate had been sealed the moment Andrew walked out of the CBS building. Never, and I mean never, have I ever encountered such a vengeful wrath come down on any show I had worked on. That was Les. Seething at Andrew's impertinence and lack of loyalty to him and Bruce, he reacted with swift finality.

For Bruce, it was the best thing that ever happened to him. He was now able to give *Drew Carey* his undivided attention. The show would run for ten seasons and make Bruce a multi-millionaire many times over. Bruce went on to create 100 episodes of the Charlie Sheen show *Anger Management* and 120 episodes of *George Lopez*.

Bruce even made up with Roseanne Barr and, in 2017, was hired to run the reimagining of *Roseanne*. Bruce got the last laugh there as well. Roseanne also self-destructed, getting herself fired. The show resurfaced yet again, this time as *The Connors*.

Now past seventy, Bruce Helford is still in demand and will be until he draws his last breath. If anyone can beat Norman Lear's longevity record, I am betting on Bruce.

As you can imagine, many people reveled in Andrew's cancellation. Undaunted, he gradually bounced back yet again. He was terrific in the HBO series *Entourage* and fabulous in Woody Allen's film *Blue*

Jasmine. He even starred in his own Showtime series, aptly enough called *Dice*, playing a Vegas comic who had self-destructed. He topped off his comeback appearing as Lady Gaga's father in *A Star is Born*.

Bless This House was a wonderful concept for a show with great stars and terrific writers. Unfortunately, the immovable object met the unstoppable force, which inevitably caused the show's demise.

Never an industry to forget a good idea, CBS resurrected the show in a slightly different form several years later. The married couple was now living in New York rather than New Jersey, and the blue-collar lead character worked at the International Parcel Service rather than the US Post Service. The show ran for nine seasons and was called *The King of Queens.*

I think they should have called it *Poetic Justice.*

"It's a touchy situation." Andrew "Dice" Clay and Cathy Moriarty on the set of Bless This House. (PF Collection)

My good luck charms, the incomparable Marty Nedboy (l) and Jimmie Briscoe in a scene with the Diceman! (PF Collection)

Executive Producer Billy Van Zandt (l) and Andrew Dice Clay, flank Dice's co-star Cathy Moriarty and Billy's writing partner Jane Milmore. (Courtesy of Billy Van Zandt)

"THE TOP TV SHOWS IN RUSSIA ARE BOWLING FOR FOOD AND WHEEL OF TORTURE."

— Yakov Smirnoff

Chapter 8

HEAD OF THE CLASS
GOES TO MOSCOW

In 1986, I had a career breakthrough. After stumbling along paying the bills by doing commercials, I landed a job on my first network series, *Head of the Class*. The ABC comedy starred Howard Hesseman as Charlie Moore, a New York City teacher of an eccentric class of gifted students in the advanced Individual Honors Program. We shot 114 episodes over five years. After the fourth season, Hesseman was replaced by Scottish comic Billy Connolly, who we would later spin off to his own show, *Billy*.

It was a great job. I learned a lot. Little did I suspect I was about to take a master class in production.

Prior to our third season, my bosses, Rich Eustis and Michael Elias, casually asked me, "What if we start next season with a rematch of our season one debate with the Russian high school team? Only this time we shoot it in the Soviet Union?"

I gulped, knowing that no one from the West had ever even attempted shooting in the Soviet Union before. It would be a daunting task. I encouraged my bosses to go for it. Somehow, we'd figure out a way to accomplish the production side. Who cared that no American had ever shot anything in Moscow before?

Warner Bros. Television and ABC thought enough of the idea to finance a fact-finding trip.

In those days getting into the Soviet Union required an official invitation from the government. Before a visa application could be accepted and issued, it had to be filed either through the Soviet embassy in Washington, D.C., or their consulate in San Francisco.

Once inside the Soviet Union, there would be no shortage of bureaucracy. Plenty of people love to say no. Finding someone to say yes is the trick.

We found a Soviet citizen living in Vienna who put us on the right track. Masha Klein directed us to her partner, Alexander Kart, a Soviet production manager with connections to the inner circle of the Soviet filmmaking community. Klein and Kart would prove essential to our project.

Kart set up a meeting with our government sponsor, SovinFilm, a bureau of the Soviet film industry that arranges joint ventures. With the meeting set for March 2, Steve Papazian and I, along with creators Eustis and Elias, set off for the USSR via Austria. When we hooked up with Klein in Vienna, she processed our visas and joined the four of us en route to Moscow.

We arrived in the Soviet Union on time and without incident. The terminal, a huge, unlit warehouse, functioned only to allow passengers to arrive and depart. Armed guards with automatic rifles were there to meet every flight. Landing in the country President Reagan only years before had called "the evil empire" was an intimidating experience to say the least.

Once we passed through customs, we met Alexander Kart.

Within the hour, we knew we had hired the right man. In a city where everyone drove a government-issue white Volga, Kart drove a navy blue Mercedes. In a city where people wore anything they could get, Kart wore designer clothes. In a city where people lined up for hours in hopes of procuring fruit, vegetables, or vodka, Kart seemed to have a limitless supply of anything and everything.

Remember, before *glasnost*, Moscow wasn't open to the West. Soviet citizens couldn't travel abroad and only knew what their government told them.

Prior to our trip, Papazian and I had prepared a list of equipment and services we would need for the proposed eight-day shoot. Based on the story outline, our agenda was to meet Wednesday with Alexander Surikov, the head of SovinFilm, then scout locations for several days. Our last day, Eustis and Elias would audition Soviet actors while Papazian and I would negotiate the production deal with Surikov.

The meeting with SovinFilm went without a hitch. From day one, the Soviets could not have been more hospitable or supportive.

As one might expect, shooting in the Soviet Union was, well, uh, different. The government ran a one-stop production supermarket. You told them what you need—how many actors, how many locations, how many rooms for how many days, how many crew, how many trucks, you name it—then you negotiated the price.

After meeting with Mosfilm, a major Soviet studio, we realized the equipment we needed—such as a generator, crane, grip apparatus, and lights—would not be compatible with our gear or standards. Everything would have to be shipped from the States.

At that meeting, the Soviets also offered us their financial proposal. Papazian and I knowingly looked at each other and smirked. Not only was their bid more than four times what we would ultimately agree on, but they also obviously had access to our US union contracts. They had attached US prices for Soviet services, right down to meal penalties.

In the Soviet Union, the maximum per month a citizen could earn in those days was 800 rubles, about $1,300. We pointed out that if this were the case and we agreed to their proposed prices, each of the 400-plus extras would make more money than Soviet President Gorbachev.

We finally agreed to pay SovinFilm ten rubles a day, about $16 per extra, and came away with an arrangement that we believed fell within the budget constraints of ABC and Warner Bros.

In April, Warner's and ABC gave their okay. We set our schedule for eight days of shooting with a July 21 departure from Los Angeles.

We still had two major hitches, a writers' strike and no script.

All we had was a three-page outline written before the March 7 strike. Prepping eleven time zones away is difficult enough, but without a script—before cell phones, computers, and the internet—we had problems that they don't teach in film schools.

During pre-production prepping, we ran into a variety of snags. It took nearly two hours to place a call to the Soviet Union, and none of the Soviet production personnel spoke English. We had to call Klein in Vienna, who in turn relayed our questions to Kart in Moscow.

Faxes were another problem.

Due to a shortage of fax paper, it sometimes took two to three days for a fax to reach its destination in the USSR. Then there was the "force majeure" clause, an unforeseeable circumstance clause in the contract between Warner's and SovinFilm.

Because of the writers' strike, we insisted on a "force majeure" clause to protect us should the walkout continue past our projected shoot date, but every time we inserted the clause, SovinFilm deleted it. Finally, I called Klein in Vienna to explain that without that clause, we had no deal.

Klein called back the next day. SovinFilm had been deleting the references to labor unions and work stoppages because they thought we were talking about a Soviet labor strike. According to Klein, "There are no such things in the Soviet Union." They reinstated the clause.

As the writers' strike continued, we had no alternative but to work toward the July 21 departure date. We finally set the weekend of July 4 as our deadline. If the strike was resolved by then, we could still meet our schedule. Hotel reservations were made. Flights were set. Paperwork was processed.

No settlement was reached that weekend. The trip had to be postponed.

By mid-July, I felt apprehensive about us pulling this off without a script, especially after only one brief pre-production outing to Moscow. I voiced my concern to Eustis and Elias, who asked if a second trip would help. I said it would, if they could write a script around the sites we picked on the trip—if and when they would be able to write a script at all.

They agreed to work around the locations and approached Harvey Shephard, then Warner Bros. Television president, about the return trip, which was not in the budget. Shephard green-lighted it, and once again, we were packing for Russia.

Director Eric Laneuville, Eustis, Elias, Papazian, and I set off to Moscow on August 1 to lock locations for a show without a script. The second trip was a godsend. The strike ended while we were in Moscow. Now, we could at last set film dates and discuss actual locations.

After Warner's and ABC said it was still a go, we had to find out if the Soviets still had lodging. Moscow was visited by hundreds of thousands of sightseers every summer.

When a tourist visited the Soviet Union, the government assigned you a hotel. We had requested the Rossiya, a 4,000-room hotel that faces Red Square. Could we still get the eighty-five rooms that we had reserved previously on short notice? As luck would have it, we could. Despite all this, if the writer's strike hadn't ended by the third week of August, there still would be no "first show in Moscow."

The shooting schedule was set for nine days in September, and rather than kick off the season, this episode would air as a one-hour special during the November sweeps. Sweeps are a big deal in Hollywood, a three-week period twice a year (the other being May) when the ratings are measured. They go a long way toward determining a show's future fate. After we shot our season opener in the States on August 26, all thoughts focused full-time on the Soviet Union.

Having completed the bureaucratic Olympics in July—only to have the 154-day writers' strike deny us—preparing to go to Moscow for the third time seemed relatively easy, especially with a script. True to their word, Eustis and Elias provided a script fashioned around the agreed-upon sites, and they had it by the end of August, three weeks after the strike had ended.

We flew all our personnel and equipment through Finnair. with a stopover in Helsinki. This was the only direct flight from Los Angeles to Moscow. We traveled in three waves: producers and director in wave one, director of photography Rich Brown and department heads in wave two, and the rest of our ranks—now swelled to nearly ninety—in wave three.

We impatiently set off in wave one, but once there, reality set in. While Eustis, Elias, and Laneuville needed an additional week to cast Soviet actors, Steve and I were left to finalize the production details. The script and shooting schedule were written in English, so they were useless, but that wasn't our biggest problem. In March and August, all requests had been "*nyet* problem," but the Soviets sang a different song in September.

"We don't think we can do that."

I sat down with a group of Soviet coordinators, assistant directors, and production managers whom I would come to fondly call the Gang of Eight. No sooner were formal introductions completed than Klein, acting as interpreter, told me that shooting the sixty-five-page script in eight days with twenty locations was "impossible."

She said we would have to cut it back. Neither Eustis, Elias, Warner Bros., nor ABC had said cut it back, so we weren't about to do it for the Soviets.

The script wasn't the only problem.

According to the Gang of Eight, it was "impossible" to cater for a combined 260 Americans and Soviets, day in and day out. It was "impossible" to find anything resembling a ten-ton truck. It was "impossible" to work extras or drivers more than eight hours at a stretch. It was "impossible" to keep our trucks at the hotel overnight, and no driver would report to work before 8 a.m.

Oh, and by the way, that was a mighty big generator we had sent. It would be "impossible" to unload 4,500 pounds. No forklift was big enough in Moscow. And, there was no way to feed it the gas it needed to run. *Nyet, nyet, nyet*, sang the chorus, yet our requests had all been made and approved many months before.

If I aged any in Moscow, that was the day. During our meeting, I came to the most important decision I'd make while in the Soviet Union.

In the USSR, you were whomever the government said you were. You drove a government-assigned car, lived in a government-assigned home, worked at a government-assigned job, and were paid a government-assigned wage.

In this socialist system, there was little incentive, and without incentive, there can't be motivation. I suspected that whenever the Soviets said, "We can't do that," they really meant they didn't want to do that.

Sometimes, of course, they really couldn't, but we'd have to determine that on the fly. For now, we'd insist that anything conceivable in concept was possible logistically. And Kart had plenty of motivation. That Mercedes wasn't bought on ten rubles a day.

With few exceptions, my hunch proved right. While we had to house one driver at our hotel, and the camera truck had to go back every evening after unloading, Kart and his Gang of Eight came through time after time. As for that 4,500-pound generator? The day after "Production Summit One," Kart walked in with a big smile and told Klein, "The generator is off the truck."

"How did you manage that?" I questioned.

"Don't ask," Kart responded, his smile spreading wider.

By now, our second wave had arrived from the States, and events moved fairly smoothly. This false sense of security vanished with the coming of the third wave.

Our final group of seventy arrived at the Warner Bros. Ranch, 1 p.m., Thursday, September 8, ready for a 6 p.m. departure from Los Angeles. Little did anyone know then that they wouldn't arrive at 5:30 p.m. Moscow time the following day as scheduled but instead well past midnight nearly three days later.

The flight from L.A. to Helsinki stayed on schedule. When it landed in Finland, our associate producer Bari Halle was informed that the

Helsinki-to-Moscow flight was overbooked. Only six of our group could fly. The remaining fifty-four would have to wait five hours in Helsinki and be split up. Some would fly Finnair, the others the official Soviet airline, Aeroflot. The earliest anyone would arrive in Moscow would be 10:30 p.m., Friday.

Remember, in those years, no one had cell phones.

Yet the quick-thinking Halle still managed to contact me in Moscow, so I was ready for the first group. We had made special provisions for technical director Chuck Reilly to take cameras and lenses on the plane. When the six people debarked, no Reilly. When the baggage came through, no cameras.

I was worried but naturally assumed the cameras would be with Reilly. While there was some initial concern, I knew that even if the cameras were lost, we still had time to ship additional cameras from West Germany. Germany, as you may recall, was still divided between a communist East and a democratic West.

I hoped I could, anyway, because when Reilly arrived on the second flight, he realized immediately that we didn't have the cameras. We soon discovered they weren't on his flight.

Thirty minutes later, Aeroflot landed with a truly dispirited band on board, only made worse by the interminable time it took to get through baggage claim. After forty-five minutes, the luggage stopped coming altogether. Not only were there still no cameras, but at nearly midnight, at least twenty people were missing luggage.

Kart interceded with a SovinFilm liaison to please have the airline check again. Bingo! The luggage handlers had curiously forgotten that there were two sides to the plane. Cameras, lenses, sound equipment, and luggage soon materialized.

Around 12:30 a.m., our weary, hungry travelers finally trudged off to the Hotel Rossiya. We were at last all accounted for. For the next ten days, this would be home. Included in that group of passengers were Robin Givens and her husband, heavyweight boxing champion of the world, Mike Tyson. Mike had recently wrapped his car around a pole, and his hand was in a cast. I suggested Robin bring Mike to help him avoid the spotlight. Little did I suspect that all three Moscow network bureaus would cover Mike's arrival. The unwanted publicity was another problem we would have to deal with.

By Saturday we had resolved our trucking problem. Although the vehicles assigned to us were vintage World War II, the problem of the generator's gas tank was solved thanks to an old fifty-five-gallon drum and some garden hose.

We were finally ready.

By 7:30 the next day, as the sun rose over the Kremlin, we were rehearsing in Red Square. It was a magnificent sight—St. Basil's Cathedral, Lenin's Tomb, and the red brick walls of the Soviet halls of government contrasting with the gold-leaf, onion-domed cathedrals.

Some logistical problems popped up along the way. Crowd control was minimal that first day. Groups of tourists sometimes meandered through the middle of scenes. Fortunately, we had scheduled shooting early enough to have most of the day's pages shot before lunch.

Ah, lunch.

Since catering on location was a somewhat novel concept to the Soviets, lunch evolved into something out of a Marx Brothers film. Here's how Chico might explain it.

Monday, the caterers showed up. Okay, but they ran out of food before everyone ate.

Tuesday, the food showed up, but on the wrong side of the Kremlin—we never found them and ended up eating at a restaurant.

Wednesday, the food showed up at the right spot, but we'd been held up shooting at our first location.

Thursday, the food didn't show up again. Kart took me to check out a restaurant and arranged a meal—soup, meat, vegetable, and ice cream.

"What kind of meat?" I asked.

"Nice meat," Kart replied.

"But what kind of meat?" I pressed.

"Good meat," said Kart. "Liver."

Fortunately, the caterer arrived.

On one of those days, Tyson, Papazian and I were standing in Red Square. Mike noticed a line as long as the eye could see to get into Lenin's Tomb.

"Waas dat?" asked Mike, with his unmistakable lisp.

"Lenin's Tomb," I said.

"Who's Lenin?" He asked.

"Lenin was sort of the George Washington of the USSR," I explained. "His mummified body is on display in there. People come from all over the country to pay their respects."

Mike's eyes lit up in childlike innocence. With his high-pitched voice, he squealed, "Leth go sthee the stiff."

We grabbed Kart, cut in front of literally a mile of people, and went into the tomb. As we descended into the cool, darkened recesses of the catacombs, I could sense Mike's anticipation building. I wish you could have seen Tyson's face when he saw what was left of Lenin. A crudely preserved face and head dressed in an empty Soviet uniform lying in state. You would have thought Mike had seen a ghost. Well, I guess he sort of did.

Following the day's shooting, each night I'd meet with the Gang of Eight to firm up the next day's schedule. But, inevitably, whenever we showed up at our designated location, the guard in charge would ask, in Russian, "Who are you?"

Don't get me wrong. The Soviets knocked themselves out to make this shoot happen. Take extras, for example. If we needed a soldier, they'd grab a soldier off the street. In one scene, two of our students were being chased by police. For the policemen, we used two Soviet militiamen assigned to us for security.

And then there were props. Our prop master, Jasper Ehrig Jr. was assigned a Soviet named Igor. Igor was a stoic in the true sense of the word, never speaking but always coming through. We were preparing to shoot a scene at the Novodevichy Convent, where our character Simone, played by Khrystyne Haje, wanted to leave flowers on the grave of Russian author Anton Chekhov. Igor was to provide the bouquet but was missing in action.

I tried to assure Ehrig that Igor would show, but he was unconvinced. As our bus pulled up to the convent, so did a police car with lights flashing and sirens wailing. Out stepped Igor, holding the flowers. *Nyet* problem.

Another time we were scheduled to shoot a scene at a sidewalk café. We needed six or seven tables and about twenty-seven chairs. We showed up, and of course, there were no tables and chairs. "*Nyet* problem" replied the Gang of Eight, who walked to an outdoor eating area about fifty yards away and took tables and chairs out from under thirty or so diners.

Nyet problem indeed.

The longer we worked with the Soviets, the smoother communications became. As the cast and crew will tell you, the days didn't get any shorter or easier, but our ability to endure them sure did. The Gang of Eight survived an uprising by their drivers—complaints about seventeen-hour workdays—and we survived cold, damp weather in somewhat cramped quarters.

We were never denied permission to shoot anything or anywhere, and by day five, even the catering crisis had been solved. Heck, even the hoopla around Tyson had died down. That would all start over again when Robin threw Mike under the bus with Barbara Walters in a *20/20 interview* That is a story for another book and another writer.

When all was said and done, we made our schedule and stuck to the budget. The show was a success, as more than 30 million viewers proved that November. Think about that for a second—30 million people.

Compare that, if you will, to the 18 million who watched the finale of *The Big Bang Theory,* the number one show on television in May 2019.

Soviet General Secretary Mikhail Gorbachev was named *Time* magazine Man of the Year in 1988. I hope Klein, Kart, and the Gang of Eight received a few votes too.

History making first day of production at St. Basil's Cathedral in Moscow. (PF Collection)

Jeanetta Arnette in front of St Basil's. (PF Collection)

Actress Kimberly Russell and the changing of the guards at Lenin's Tomb. (PF Collection)

Sascha Kart (l) and two members of his infamous gang of eight. (PF Collection)

With Executive Producer Rich Eustis, Associate Producer Bari Halle, and my mentor, Steve Papazian, Warner Bros. VP of Production in Red Square. (PF Collection)

"THE BEST IS ALWAYS FRAGILE."

— Sugar Ray Robinson

Chapter 9

SUDDENLY SUSAN –
A STAR-CROSSED SHOW

"Hello, Frank," the polite voice said. "This is Donald Trump. What can I do for you?"

I had the real estate magnate on the phone and was trying to get him to make a guest appearance on *Suddenly Susan*. I almost found the conversation diverting. I needed the break. It had been a long couple of months laden with turmoil.

The year had been bittersweet. Usually the table read for a pilot is cause for great celebration, yet the day of *Suddenly Susan's*, I was consumed with grief.

My sleep had been interrupted at 1 a.m. by Rod Carew's phone call summoning me to the hospital for his eighteen-year-old daughter, Michelle.

The horrific jolt bolted me from my bed and had me racing to Anaheim. The car had made this trip so many times it was as if it drove itself. At 5:30 a.m. that terrible Wednesday morning, Michelle's courageous seven-month battle against cancer had come to an end.

The family held a press conference at 7:30 a.m., and an hour-and-a-half later, I was back at Warner Bros. Less than three hours later, the table read completed, I knew it was useless. My mind couldn't focus on work, so I shot back to the hospital to be with the Carew's.

Suddenly Susan was bittersweet in so many ways.

The turmoil was just beginning.

The story revolved around Susan Keane, a San Francisco magazine reporter who had left her fiancé at the altar.

Suddenly she was just Susan.

Clyde Phillips had created the hit *Parker Lewis Can't Lose* and visualized Susan as a single-camera show. NBC told Clyde that if he could get Brooke Shields or Julie Warner to star as Susan that they would make the pilot. Clyde got Brooke to commit; whereupon, NBC and Warner Bros. changed the show to a multi-camera comedy, two totally different disciplines. That move promptly got Clyde sacked.

To run the reconceived show and write the pilot, they brought in old pals Billy Van Zandt and Jane Milmore. In addition to Brooke, the show would star Maggie Wheeler, Elizabeth Ashley, David Krumholtz, Phil Casnoff, and two-time Emmy Award winner Nancy Marchand as Grandma.

On an interesting side note, not only was Nancy Marchand later on *The Sopranos* as Tony's Mom Livia, but Billy Van Zandt's brother, Little Steven, also co-starred on *The Sopranos*, though he is better known as the lead guitarist for Bruce Springsteen's E Street Band.

When the show finally got picked up, everyone but Brooke and I got fired. The network wanted more "subtle" writers than Billy and Jane. As for the actors, no one really popped in testing. So, now we were in our *third* rendition, inspiring us to sarcastically call the show "Eventually Susan."

With former *Murphy Brown* writers Steve Peterman and Gary Dontzig, who I had become good friends with, now running the show, NBC and Warner's finally hit the jackpot. The new cast included Nestor Carbonell, Judd Nelson, Kathy Griffin, David Strickland, Andrea Bendewald, and Barbara Barrie as Grandma.

Barbara was hired to replace Nancy Marchand, whose late-stage cancer had caused her to fail the Warner Bros. insurance physical. Nancy would go on to win two more Emmys for *The Sopranos* while on oxygen—the second posthumously in 2000.

Suddenly Susan's star Brooke Shields had married tennis great Andre Agassi, who became a constant presence on the stage. The craft service lady, Shirley, would make Andre grilled cheese sandwiches, and Andre would tip her $20. Everyone else went hungry when Andre was around.

When the show premiered, Andre sent his charter jet to Burbank to pick up the cast and my wife and me. We all flew to Vegas to view the first episode and have a barbeque before flying home. Andre's jet wasn't a compact either. It was a full-bore "fly me to Wimbledon nonstop—I have to get my sleep in a king-sized bed" jet.

We shot in front of a live audience. Brooke was such a big star we changed the show's taping from 7: 30 p.m. to 5 o'clock. "You are crazy—you'll never get an audience that early, too much traffic," we were told.

"Watch," I said confidently, "Brooke is such a big star they will come out to see her if we shoot at noon." Come they did, in huge numbers.

The show skyrocketed with the help of some amazing executives at NBC. David Nevins went on to become president of Showtime and CBS. The erudite John Landgraf became president of the FX Network and was later dubbed by the media the unofficial Mayor of Television. Jamie Tarses became president of ABC.

Carrie Burke, the current president of ABC, and Robin Schwartz, then president of the Oprah Winfrey Network, now executive producer of Fox's *Central Park,* all cut their teeth on *Susan* during our four-year run. It was an embarrassment of riches.

We premiered behind *Friends* and finished number three for the season. When *Friends* aired a repeat a few weeks later, we vaulted to number one.

Brooke Shields was absolutely fabulous.

As funny as everyone in the cast was, and they were real pros, Brooke shined. The first thing you noticed about her was that despite the beauty she displayed on film and television, no camera had ever done her justice. She was an example of nature perfecting itself, yet she would fearlessly wrestle Hulk Hogan and would think nothing of taking a pie in the face. In short anything for a laugh.

One week, Kathy Griffin was being a pain in the ass. Sometimes we would pre-shoot a scene one day in advance to avoid a big makeup change on show night. This was one of those days.

Kathy's character, Vicki, was in a bar in Mexico flirting with the handsome barkeeper who didn't speak English. Prior to her departure from San Francisco, where the show was set, Vicki had been very dismissive of Luis's (Nestor Carbonell) Cuban accent. In the next breath, she had asked Luis for something sexy to say if she met a man.

To set her up, Luis told her something totally inappropriate. The scene called for Vicki to tell the bartender what Luis had told her, and the barkeep would throw a drink in her face.

All week we rehearsed that scene.

Kathy would say the words, but obviously during rehearsal, the actor playing the barkeep wouldn't throw the drink. Come shooting time, Kathy refused to get hit with the drink. I was called to the stage.

"What's the problem?" I asked.

"I am not getting hit in the face with that drink," she said.

"You've known about it all week."

"I don't care. I am not getting hit with that drink."

I was losing patience. The crew was looking on. We were burning clock, and I wasn't about to have my authority challenged by Kathy Griffin.

"Tell you what," I said. "If you can honestly tell me that Brooke wouldn't take that drink to the face, then you don't have to take the drink to the face."

Kathy took the drink to the face.

As the show got more and more successful, Griffin's behavior got worse. At the beginning of year three, she went to Steve and Gary and griped that she was who was making Brooke funny.

She constantly demanded more storylines and screen time. Steve and Gary patiently explained that she was doing what a supporting actress is supposed to do, support the star. Still, she never stopped bitching. Much later, Kathy committed career suicide when she was photographed holding the aforementioned severed head of President Trump. She would never again reach the heights she did on *Suddenly Susan*.

Regarding my phone call with Trump, he did agree to appear on *Suddenly Susan*. In separate episodes, so did President Gerald Ford's son and Presidential candidate Senator Bob Dole, only months after losing the election to Bill Clinton.

Dole was a delightful guest. People came from all over the lot to have their pictures taken with him. He stayed for more than an hour to accommodate everyone.

I asked his chief of staff, "Where was that guy on the campaign trail?"

"You're seeing the real Bob Dole," he said. "The guy on the campaign trail was the guy Republican bosses thought he should be."

But it was Trump who resonated with me. Trump was a trip.

I had called Trump's office to inquire about the possibility of him appearing in a pre-shot scene in which magazine publisher Jack Richman (Judd Nelson) hosts a weekly card game with a few friends. Brooke got us tennis great John McEnroe. We cast San Francisco Mayor Willie Brown and added Mr. T as the third.

I had pitched Steve and Gary the idea of Donald Trump as the fourth. They said if you can get him, they would absolutely write him in. So, I set out to make it happen. It was easier than it should have been. The conversation went something like this.

"Donald Trump's office, may I help you?" the secretary said.

"Mr. Trump, please," I said.

"I am sorry. He's not available."

"Can you tell him that Frank Pace called and ask him to return my call? I am the producer of *Suddenly Susan,* and we would like him to appear in an episode."

"Can you hold on, please?"

"Hello, Frank," the man said. "This is Donald Trump. What can I do for you?"

While I was telling Brooke the story of how I had booked Donald, I thought I detected a glint of discomfort in her eyes.

"I hope I didn't make a mistake," I said.

"No," she said. "It's just that one time in New York, I had an uncomfortable experience with him. I am sure he's over it by now."

Steve and Gary did indeed write a part for Trump's character. In the episode, Vicki holds up an aptly titled *Skazzy* magazine with Donald's picture on the cover with the headline, "Our Next President?"

It was 1997.

The Monday after the show taped, Brooke came up to me with a shit-eating grin on her face.

"Well, we are two for two with The Donald, but this time I was ready for him."

I didn't press for details.

Steve and Gary were antsy to create their own show. They had not created *Murphy Brown* nor *Suddenly Susan.* Diane English and Clyde Phillips had. The duo were hot writers rightfully looking for their pot of gold at the end of the syndication rainbow.

Suddenly Susan's evolving plot had Susan and her editor Jack Richmond develop a relationship. When they consummated it midway through season three, just like that all the sexual tension between the two dissipated. We were doomed.

Doomed as we thought we were then, we were about to go down for the count.

David Strickland was a brilliant talent, but his demons included bipolar disorder and a long history of addictions. Unbeknownst to us, he was arrested between seasons two and three for possession of cocaine. He pleaded no contest and was sentenced to three years' probation.

One Friday, he reminded me that he was due in court the following Monday for a progress report. He promised me, however, that he would absolutely make the table read.

He didn't.

Early Monday morning, an ashen Steve and Gary walked into my office. They had just received a call from Las Vegas detectives. It appeared Strickland and comic Andy Dick had flown from Los Angeles to Las Vegas and spent three days partying. After checking into a room at the Oasis Motel, Strickland spent time with a prostitute, consumed a six-pack of beer, and hung himself with a bedsheet.

So much promise, gone.

It fell to Steve and me to tell the cast. David had become Brooke's best friend. This would be hard. We jammed all the performers into Brooke's small dressing room. They sensed Steve and I were not there to share anything positive. But they weren't expecting the horrible news we were about to deliver.

The cast responded first with gasps, followed by uncontrollable wailing. Suffice to say, it was heartbreaking. We suspended the last two shows of the season before returning for one last tribute episode to David.

Steve and Gary left for greener pastures. On came the fourth set of writers. They were replaced by the shotgun marriage of Maria Semple and Mark Driscoll to Chris Vane, who had been elevated from the previous staff. The three hadn't worked together before and didn't share the same vision for the show. Driscoll had some cache, having written the classic episode of *Ellen* in which Ellen DeGeneres publicly declared herself to be gay.

Mark quickly proved to be an amiable but ineffective fellow. So ineffective in fact that I forgot he was even an executive producer in the first draft of this book. Maria Semple, who went on to become a successful novelist, apparently wasn't even a big believer of our show. A Kathy Griffin fan, she replaced half the cast and changed the sets the fans had gotten comfortable with. The show might have survived one of those changes with our audience, but two were too much to ask for.

She further sabotaged Chris by replacing Steve and Gary's staff with writers that blew in whatever direction she did. Despite the addition of Eric Idle and Sherri Shepherd to the cast, the newer show looked and felt contrived. Brooke gamely tried to make it through, but as good as she continued to be, it was over.

Suddenly Susan essentially had died with David Strickland.

Executive Producer Steven Peterman and Gary Dontzig (standing) delivered big guest stars to Suddenly Susan such as (r-l) Rose Marie, Harvey Korman, and Tim Conway, along with, of course, Brooke. (Courtesy of Steve Peterman)

...and the legendary Tony Bennett here in a PR photo from the show with Brooke. (PF Collection)

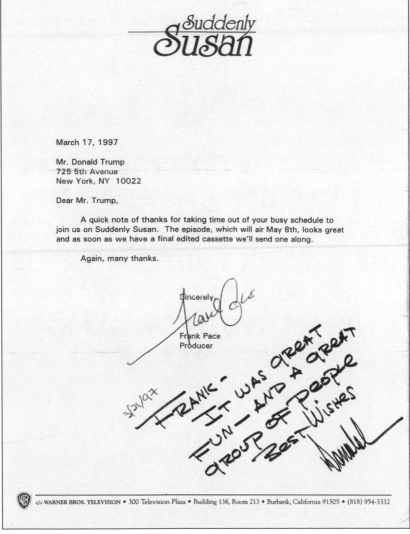

Suddenly Susan

March 17, 1997

Mr. Donald Trump
725 5th Avenue
New York, NY 10022

Dear Mr. Trump,

A quick note of thanks for taking time out of your busy schedule to join us on Suddenly Susan. The episode, which will air May 8th, looks great and as soon as we have a final edited cassette we'll send one along.

Again, many thanks.

Sincerely

Frank Pace
Producer

FRANK - IT WAS GREAT FUN - AND A GREAT GROUP OF PEOPLE Best Wishes

c/o WARNER BROS. TELEVISION • 300 Television Plaza • Building 136, Room 213 • Burbank, California 91505 • (818) 954-3332

AND, oh yeah, Donald Trump. (Mitchell Haddad Photography)

"OVER THE COURSE OF MY
FIFTY-YEAR CAREER, I DID
SIXTY FILMS. EACH OF THOSE
FILMS TOOK THREE MONTHS.
SO BASICALLY, I WAS
UNEMPLOYED FOR ALMOST
FORTY YEARS."

– Jack Lemmon

Chapter 10

AN ACTOR'S LIFE

I have been a producer now for almost forty years. One thing I can say for certain is the last job I would want on a movie set is working actor. Don't get me wrong. There are a lot worse jobs in life than an actor. Few, however, have crueler career choices.

If you succeed, the profession can be rewarding, but success can be harder than running a marathon in high heels. Even if you're lucky enough to survive, the odds are you still won't be able to support yourself. When I was younger, our offices were off-site. One time, a veteran actor I was walking to the stage with randomly asked, "You know the longest walk you will ever have to make in your career?"

I shook my head no.

"The walk from this side of the street to that side," he said, pointing to the studio entrance.

Only a select few make a living acting. The frustration most of them suffer before having even limited success boggles the brain.

Think about it.

Some 150,000 members of the Screen Actors Guild-American Federation of Television and Radio Artists (SAG-AFTRA) pay union dues. That includes dancers, stuntmen, stand-ins, etc. Of the 150,000 dues-paying members, fewer than five percent make more than $100,000 per year, and only 15 percent qualify for annual medical benefits. The majority gross less than $30,000 per year.

If the above statistics don't dampen your desire to frolic in the footlights, then consider the grueling audition process you'll have to endure on your way to the lofty goal of perpetual unemployment.

You can't get an audition without an agent, but you can't get an agent without a union card. That sounds simple enough. Yet you can't join the union until you have worked in a union-affiliated production.

Talk about a catch-22.

The audition usually involves fifteen to twenty people, all about the same age, height, and weight and typically the same sex. The contenders crowd a casting office's waiting room to "read" for a part. The actor usually reads one or two scenes for the role while the casting director sits in for the star.

The hopefuls may have had overnight to prepare but more than likely have had only two to three hours to study the material they are performing. The director, the executive producer, the producer, and the casting director summon the swarm of actors one by one into a sterile space to read for that single part.

As a producer, I always hope the contenders succeed. After all, my goal is to cast the part. Truth is, we producers aren't even sure what we are looking for. We're hoping the actors show us.

Our basic rule is to first see what the actor's interpretation of the material is before we attempt any direction. Anyone can take direction. We want to see what they believe in. The good stuff always comes from the heart.

Actors typically pour out their souls performing the scene, only to hear, "Thank you. That was terrific." After every audition, they hear the same robotic "terrific," over and over again. Try paying your rent with "terrifics."

There are no courtesy rejection calls in this business. If twenty people audition, only whoever wins the part gets a call, and the casting director calls the actor's agent, not the actor, to deliver the good news and to finalize "The Deal."

The majority of actors find work as guest stars on weekly television shows. With episodic television, "The Deal" is really no big deal. A speaking part in a union production pays $975 per day. At Warner Bros., a weekly five-day rate for a thirty-minute episode, "top of show" actor pays approximately $5,418 (as of 2020).

From that, the actor pays a 10 percent agent fee and maybe another 5 percent to a manager, not to mention whatever is owed to Uncle Sam, who always gets his cut.

That's it.

Sure, an Ed Sheeran will earn more to guest on *Game of Thrones,* as will an Oprah Winfrey to guest star on *30 Rock* or a Bette Midler on *Murphy Brown.*

But those are exceptions—and rare exceptions at that.

Now consider that an actor may be rejected at twenty to thirty or forty auditions between "jobs." Then realize how many jobs even at $5,418 a week the actor has to do to reach America's mean income of $56,000 per year.

You can see the difficulty both psychologically and financially for a "working" actor, yet as Jimmy Durante memorably echoed while shaking his head in exasperation, "Everybody wants to get into the act."

Why does the profession's alleged glamour, the appeal of applause, and the promise of fame and fortune lure so many unsuspecting lambs toward inevitable slaughter and heartbreak? One can't just help but wonder why? The only answer I keep coming up with is that it beats growing up!

One must understand how difficult it is to get work to fully appreciate how rewarding having a steady gig means to most actors. Especially for those actors lucky enough to land a series. To those fortunate few, a hit series may come along once in a lifetime.

George Clooney was cast in ten failed pilots or series before finding stardom in *ER*. Stephen Lang struggled to make ends meet for twenty-five years before landing the role of Colonel Miles Quaritch in director James Cameron's *Avatar,* the highest-grossing movie of all time. Cameron had remembered Stephen from an audition ten years prior.

And admit it, as great of an actor as Steve is, you still had to Google him before you had your aha moment of recognition.

Stephen once told me, "I start the new year with one goal, making my nut financially." Now he's shooting *Avatar 2, 3,* and *4* on a 1000-day schedule in Los Angeles and New Zealand. Stephen doesn't have to worry about his nut anymore. Most actors are not so fortunate.

While those privileged enough to costar on a hit series can earn in excess of $250,000 annually, the majority toil in relative anonymity, portraying the star's father, mother, best friend, sassy secretary, or wacky neighbor before returning to the rank of working actor upon the show's inevitable cancellation.

The smart ones save their money during the windfall years. The majority, who assume the gravy train will last forever, buy and then sell their big home within a year or two after the show goes off the air. It is fun to watch the cars that cast members drive to the set their first season of a new show. They start off driving three to twenty-year-old Kias, Yugos, and Volkswagens. By year two, they're sporting new Lexuses, BMWs, and Mercedes.

All the comedies I have produced featured fine ensemble casts. Most of them experience actor turmoil sooner or later. One form of unrest I simply detest. The other I simply can't fathom.

In its first of two seasons, *Nikki* starring Nikki Cox was picked up on the Fox network for nine additional episodes. It triggered contractual options for each cast member. We producers wanted to exercise all the cast's options, but the network and the studio didn't agree.

As often happens with a new series, we concentrated our creative efforts on the lead stars. It's usually not until the second half of the season when the viewers get comfortable with the stars that the supporting characters start to receive more story emphasis.

That's when those characters start to pop. Marina Benedict is a terrific actress who was cast to play Nikki's best friend, Luna. After we auditioned more than 200 women in three different cities in an exhaustive search, *Nikki* was the break Marina had been waiting for. In the twelve episodes she appeared, Marina exceeded our highest hopes.

Yet because testing focus groups decided our audience was not "invested" in Luna, the network insisted her option be dropped. When the studio folded and backed the network rather than us, we were forced to concede. It broke Marina's heart. Crestfallen, Marina might have quit the business.

She persevered, though, and has worked steadily since, appearing in *Flesh and Bones, Prison Break,* and *Gotham.* Yet even Marina still finds it necessary to supplement her income as the associate chair of the dance department at the American Music and Dramatic Academy.

For Your Love, on the other hand, was subjected to a different kind of drama. Entering our fourth season, actor Edafe Blackmon, who played Reggie, showed up with a new last name (Okurume) and a strong desire to be written off the show. Now, if there is a category of world's luckiest man somewhere, Edafe would have to be high on that list.

Landing a long-running series in his first try, Edafe, a talented actor and before all this bullshit one of my cast favorites, had earned a substantial living on *For Your Love.* His job afforded him three to four months' vacation, prepared meals, and, most importantly, a steady job. Now he wanted out. Loudly.

Again, why?

I remember when I was a kid, *Bonanza* was a Sunday night ritual around our house.

One year, we tuned into the season premiere to learn that Pernell Roberts, who played the oldest Cartwright son, Adam, had left the show. My father, a self-employed piano tuner, was outraged.

"Nobody ever heard of him before *Bonanza,* and nobody will ever hear from him again," my dad predicted.

In fact, Roberts did resurface about fifteen years later as the star of *Trapper John M.D.,* but before that, I heard my dad say more than a few times, "I'll bet that horse's ass wishes he had never left *Bonanza* now."

In the '80s, my Dad's disgust was re-directed at Larry Linville (Major Frank Burns), who left *M*A*S*H* after three years to ultimately disappear onto the dinner theater circuit. "He will be sorry," my dad said. A few years later, my father saw Linville at a local public golf course waiting for his tee time. "That guy should be playing country clubs," my dad harrumphed, gratified that his prediction had come true.

"I really miss my job on *Suddenly Susan,*" said Brooke Shields. "I miss having a place to go to every day. I miss the cast and the people I worked with on the crew. I miss what most people take for granted in their everyday lives, the routine."

Holly Robinson Peete agreed with Shields, telling me, "I love knowing what I'm doing tomorrow," said the actress, who appeared on the series *21 Jump Street, Hanging with Mr. Cooper,* and *For Your Love,* over a combined fifteen consecutive seasons. Now she stars in the reality show *Meet The Peetes* and in a series of Lifetime movies.

"The consistency makes me feel secure, and the security makes me a better wife and mother. That's really what's most important to me."

What about an actor who wants off a show?

"Everybody has a different criterion for happiness," actress Robinson Peete said. "I've never been possessed by actor demons. I've always been happy with the women I've portrayed. I've never wondered what I was missing out on. There has always been enough time for me to try different roles in the three to four months of series hiatus."

Tony O'Dell understands the feast-or-famine life of an actor. "For five years I had a steady job as Alan on *Head of the Class.* Then for three years, I was unemployed, not one job. I made and sold candles to keep myself occupied. Finally, I decided if I wanted to stay in the business, I needed to expand my focus."

Today, O'Dell has established himself as one of the top dialogue coaches in the industry, having worked with the likes of Zendaya, Bella Thorne, and the actors in the film franchise *Diary of A Wimpy Kid*. He is also much in demand as a voice-over artist.

"I think a certain desperation started to come through in my auditions," said O'Dell. "Now that I have this new career, I'm more relaxed, and I'm getting acting work again." Today, Tony can be seen on the new YouTube Original TV series *Cobra Kai*, a follow-up to the classic 1982 movie in which he co-starred, *The Karate Kid*.

Let's get back to Edafe. As far as he was concerned, the studio steadfastly refused to void his contract. He decided to fight the studio with a one-man work slowdown. If Okurume showed up at all, it was hours late, and then he'd go through the motions. He literally dared Warner Bros. to fire him. Finally, the studio had enough of his shenanigans and granted his wish.

I asked Okurume, "Why, with only half a season to go, would you insist on leaving the show and more than $175,000 plus in non-recoupable salary behind?"

"I'd rather not answer that," he said, politely. "An actor has to be mysterious. He can't let the audience know what he is."

Sixteen years later, the audience not only doesn't know what he is, they don't know who he is.

Daniel Dae Kim and Grace Park had been with *Hawaii Five-O* since the beginning of the rebooted CBS series in 2010. With seven seasons behind them as supporting co-stars, the duo exited amidst a contract dispute in 2017, leaving perhaps more than $500,000 each per year on the table.

They wanted the same pay as stars Alex O'Loughlin and Scott Caan. Ultimately, CBS would not budge, so the writers wrote Kim and Park off the show. In season eight, the two had rolled the dice and came up snake eyes.

Cote de Pablo recently pulled a similar stunt. Like Okurume, she demanded to be released from the remainder of her contract. After filming nearly 200 episodes of *NCIS*, she felt the need to explore her "creative opportunities." She couldn't wait an extra year or two?

It was nice knowing you, Cote. All I can add is that I sincerely hope you saved your money.

Enduring television star Holly Robinson Peete with First Lady Michelle Obama. This job does have its perks. (PF Collection)

Tony O'Dell has transitioned from a working actor into a career as a dialogue coach, shown here with pupils Zendaya and Bella Thorne. (Courtesy of Tony O'Dell)

"A GREAT COACH WILL BEAT YOU WITH YOUR'N IN THE MORNING AND TURN AROUND AND BEAT YOU WITH HIS'N IN THE AFTERNOON."

– Bum Phillips

Chapter 11

JOHN WOODEN –
TEACHER AND COACH

How many people can say they had dinner with the best of anything? Well, I had dinner with the best coach of all time. Not just the best basketball coach of all time, the best *coach*.

Thirty-three years had passed since the five men gathering had last met in 1970. Although never formally introduced, the three hours they spent together that afternoon would link them for the rest of their lives.

Time had been good to all of them.

The dentist from Oregon, the California TV executive, the Newport Beach motivational speaker, and the Florida businessman. All four were in their fifties then. The fifth man was well into his nineties and carried those years with the wisdom of someone three times his age and the clarity of a man seventy years younger.

He calls himself a teacher first and foremost. Indeed, he is. The world, however, knows him as John Wooden, former basketball coach at UCLA and ESPN's Coach of the Century. The other four men are Dr. Vaughn Wedeking, Andy Hill, John Vallely, and basketball Hall of Fame member Artis Gilmore.

When they first connected back in March 1970, the setting was not nearly as serene, and the five men were hardly alone. Eighteen thousand screaming fans were in attendance, including me, a sophomore at Jacksonville University. That team taught me an indelible lesson that stuck with me for the remainder of my life. People from small places can accomplish big things.

We had shocked the world just by being in the NCAA Basketball Finals. The hardwood floor they collided on that afternoon was at the University of Maryland's Cole Field House. Gilmore and Wedeking wore the green and gold of the upstart JU Dolphins. Vallely and Hill suited up in blue and white for the Bruins, the perennial champions from UCLA.

A series of coincidences had made the 2003 dinner possible.

In memory of his late daughter Michelle, Carew hosts the annual Rod Carew Pediatric Cancer Research Foundation golf tournament.

Through Rod's continuing fundraising efforts, I met UCLA basketball legend John Vallely, who in 1991 had himself lost a daughter, Erin, to cancer. When John and Rod joined the Board of Directors of Southern California's PCRF, the Rod Carew Children's Cancer Golf Classic became a reality.

At the tournament, Vallely offered a private dinner for six with Coach Wooden as an auction item. There was little doubt that Rod and I would enter the winning bid—especially since Vallely was now facing his own battle with lymphoma.

There was even less doubt as to whom I would invite to join us, Dr. Vaughn Wedeking and the big fella himself, Artis Gilmore. All of us had remained close since college. When Vallely told me that dinner would be at the home of Andy Hill, the night was complete.

Having first met on a 1984 movie set, Andy and I were old friends. Andy would later become the President of CBS Productions and be responsible for the success of shows like *Dr. Quinn, Medicine Woman* and *Touched by an Angel.*

Hill himself had a curiously sour history with Wooden. Although having played on three of Wooden's national championship teams, Andy hadn't spoken a word to Wooden for twenty-five years. A hot-shot recruit when he came out of high school, Hill was still bitter that Wooden had played him so sparingly during those UCLA years.

"Andy always thought I didn't play him because I didn't like him." Wooden chuckled over dinner. "I liked Andy just fine. He didn't play because his teammates were better."

Hill would finally phone and make peace with his former mentor after he realized that the success he had achieved in his professional career was directly linked to the life lessons he had learned from Coach Wooden.

Rod and his wife Rhonda joined us at dinner.

One particular elephant still haunted the room.

As soon as the last guest arrived, Vallely spoke up and lanced the imaginary beast. "Let's get this out of the way right now, so we can get on with the evening. Sidney goaltended Artis."

All eyes turned to Wooden. His lips said nothing, but his eyes twinkled volumes, triggering a slight trace of gratifying redemption on Artis's face.

For those who don't remember that game, Jacksonville jumped out to a ten-point lead midway through the first half with Artis scoring at will. Wooden called a timeout. When UCLA returned to the floor, 6'8" forward Sidney Wicks—who went on to have an All-Star NBA career—had positioned himself behind Artis while center Steve Patterson fronted him.

Jacksonville still managed to get the ball in to Gilmore, but Wicks blocked several of Artis's shots. Lacking adjustments by JU's coaching staff, UCLA cruised to victory.

"I thought the referees were intimidated by UCLA and Coach Wooden," mused Wedeking.

"It wasn't my idea to move Wicks behind Gilmore," Wooden chuckled. "It was Sidney's. That wasn't something I would have thought of, but nothing else was working, so we gave it a try. I did tell Steve Patterson to go back and help Sidney out because individually they were overmatched."

Now, almost half a century later as I painstakingly reviewed the footage in Zapruder-like fashion for my 2017 documentary, *Jacksonville WHO?*, I was hoping to find proof of the referee's malfeasance.

The film did show Wicks had clearly goaltended Artis but not nearly as much as we JU fans had originally thought. Certainly not enough to have changed the outcome of the game.

UCLA's Vallely, the MVP of those NCAA finals, said, "Jacksonville was a big team. It had Artis, superb guards, and good depth. In the end, however, I think our forwards were quicker than their forwards, and that made the difference."

"Of the three national championships that our team won, the game against Jacksonville meant the most," Andy Hill said. We didn't think much of Florida State in '72 or Villanova in '71. Jacksonville had us scared to death."

For twelve seasons, beginning in 1964, Wooden's teams won a record ten NCAA titles, including seven in a row from '67 to '73. That was an amazing stretch in which UCLA forged what is arguably the greatest dynasty in sports history. Forget baseball's New York Yankees, college football's Notre Dame, or the NBA's Boston Celtics. All had long and sensational runs, but only Wooden's UCLA basketball dynasty had to cope with both changing rosters every year and the sudden-death format of the NCAA tournament.

Certainly, Wooden benefited from having legendary big men Lew Alcindor (Kareem Abdul Jabbar) and Bill Walton, but if you think UCLA dominated because of size, consider that Wooden's 1964 championship team rolled into the NCAAs with a 26-0 record and his tallest starter was only 6 5." In close to thirty years of coaching, his only losing season was his first at Indiana State, and his records boast of 88 consecutive wins and four perfect seasons.

The title legend makes Wooden uncomfortable. The title teacher doesn't. According to one of his greatest players, Bill Walton, "Coach Wooden never talked about winning and losing, but rather about the effort to win. He rarely talked about basketball, but generally about life. He never talked about strategy, statistics, or plays but rather about people and character. Coach never tired of telling us that once you become a good person, then you have a chance of becoming a good basketball player."

That evening we eventually set the past aside and talked of how Wooden's perspective on success had influenced our current lives, careers, and families.

"Failing to prepare is preparing to fail," "Great leaders give credit to others but accept the blame themselves," "Be quick but don't hurry" are only three of Wooden's many quoted bromides.

Wooden wouldn't let the conversation linger on his irrefutable coaching tenets. His head swiveled on his shoulders, as though he were surveying the group and wanted to move on. He preferred talking baseball with Rod Carew.

"It's my favorite sport," Wooden admitted. "So much thinking, so much strategy."

I got the feeling that if Wooden had gone into baseball, we might never have heard of Casey Stengel.

Andy and John's wives prepared our dinner. They fixed Coach's favorite meal: fried chicken, mashed potatoes, peas and carrots, biscuits with honey, and, for dessert, another Wooden favorite, blueberry pie with ice cream.

Coach led us in prayer, which was soon followed by the evening's unexpected highlight. John Vallely announced he had just finished his final chemo session and had been declared cancer-free. It gave a beautiful evening even more perspective.

After dinner, we retired to the Hill living room.

We all literally sat at Coach's feet while he slowly talked about his proudest professional accomplishment. His smile collapsed; his face suddenly rigid. He walked us through his Pyramid of Success, the cornerstones of which are "industriousness" and "enthusiasm" and at its peak are "faith" and "patience."

Wooden's pyramid took the one-time Indiana high school English teacher fourteen years to complete. He then shared with us poems he treasured followed by stories about two of his favorite historical figures, Mother Teresa and Abraham Lincoln.

The love and respect Hill and Vallely had for Wooden was obvious. They saw or spoke with him daily. Although not all UCLA alums are as close, all speak about their coach with well-documented reverence.

"Coach has become this mythical figure," said Hill. "But he was no saint. He could give it to a referee or an opposing player with the best of them. Coach was human. He had his flaws."

His sense of self is what gave his teachings their weight. Wooden hated his nickname "The Wizard of Westwood."

"I'm no wizard," he insisted. "The team with the best players almost always wins. You need talent to succeed."

There is nothing mystical about that.

It was Andy Hill who spearheaded the efforts for John Wooden to receive the Congressional Medal of Freedom from President Bush in 2003, and it was Andy who stood proudly by his mentor's side at the White House celebration.

When our evening came to an end, the elder and his now middle-aged guests rose to say their goodbyes. For thirty-three years, five of them had been bound together by one game. A game in which what they were was more important than who they were.

Now, with the innocence of youth gone and many of their future promises fulfilled, others are left forever unanswered. Everyone would head into the future with understanding and respect for the person each other had become.

The next morning, I received an email from Vallely. "Coach really had a great time last night," he said. "He was as touched that Artis and

Vaughn would travel across the country to see him as he was impressed by Artis' gentleness. And he really loved talking baseball with Rod."

Like that afternoon in March more than three decades earlier, that January evening in Los Angeles had left its mark on everyone who was there, even legendary coach John Wooden, teacher.

Pictured l-r, seated: Artis Gilmore and Coach John Wooden. Standing: Frank, Vaughn Wedeking, John Vallely, Andy Hill, and Rod Carew. (Courtesy of John Vallely)

Artis making a point during his Hall of Fame induction speech. He was presented by fellow Hall of Fame member, "Dr. J" Julius Erving. (Courtesy Naismith Memorial Basketball Hall of Fame)

At 7'2", Artis stands tall wherever he goes, here with heavyweight champ Mike Tyson (see Chapter 8). (Courtesy of Artis Gilmore)

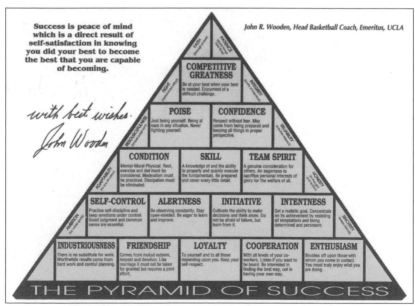

It took John Wooden fourteen years to complete his masterpiece. (Courtesy of John Wooden)

"A CAMEL IS A HORSE BUILT BY COMMITTEE."

— Howard Morris

Chapter 12

A LITTLE WILDER

All great shows are created and run by people who have singular voices. Aaron Sorkin on *The West Wing*, Diane English on *Murphy Brown*, Bruce Helford on *Drew Carey* and *George Lopez*, Chuck Lorre on the *Big Bang Theory* and *The Kominsky Method*, and Yvette Bowser on *Living Single* and *For Your Love*—all of whom are wise enough to listen to people around the writing table, but in the end, they alone determine what goes in the script. No rule by committee for them. When these visionaries create a show, the chances of a hit are greatly enhanced.

They understand you need a good story first and foremost and a good script supported by fine actors, and the creator must be prepared to fight like hell to bring his or her version of those suitable stories to the screen.

In the mid '90s, we shared the second floor of a Warner Bros. office building with creators of the show *Chicago Sons*. Ed Decter and John J. Strauss were two nice guys and really good writers. Despite wanting to do right by Warner Bros. and CBS early in their writing careers, they nevertheless found their concept canceled after only thirteen episodes.

After the axe fell, Decter and Strauss went to CBS president Les Moonves and asked in essence what the hell happened. "We took every note you gave us."

With the cold and calculating ease of the executioner he was, Les dismissed them with a curt "Maybe you should have said no to a few of them."

Ed and John learned their lesson and put it to good use, going on to write many more successful TV series and movies, including the megahit *There's Something About Mary*.

About the same time as *Chicago Sons*, NBC desperately wanted to develop a vehicle for Gene Wilder. Their coup came to fruition when they signed an agreement with the star of *The Producers, Young Frankenstein,* and *Stir Crazy.*

They shot one pilot in New York called *Eligible Dentist.* Thrilled with Gene but not with the script, NBC scrapped it. In the meantime, director Barnet Kellman, who had directed the pilots of *Murphy Brown* and *Mad About You,* had a working relationship with a New York playwright named Lee Kalcheim. Lee has an interesting personal and professional story. A successful comedy writer in the '70s, he had penned his share of episodes on Norman Lear's groundbreaking hit series *All in The Family* and *Sanford and Sons.*

In the late '80s, Lee retreated to his passion of playwriting and supplemented his income by teaching screenwriting in college. There he became smitten with a young undergraduate more than twenty years his junior. Lee fell in love with Julia, and they soon married. She blessed the fifty-two-year-old Lee with twin boys, Gabe and Sam.

It was a new and exciting time for Lee and Julia.

Lee now needed money a little more than he had in his prior fifty-two years, so he wrote a pilot script about his life, which Barnet read and liked. NBC liked it, too, and it ultimately became Gene's follow-up to *Eligible Dentist.* It was called *Something Wilder.*

The show would now be shot in L.A. Gene would play the Lee character (Gene Bergman) while Julia's character would be called Annie. The setting would be Lee's hometown of Stockbridge, Massachusetts, renowned as painter Norman Rockwell's town of residence.

Gene would be running an ad agency (something I knew all about) in his barn behind the house. Lee's story was a good old American tale of life, love, and family values, Rockwellian in every way. Ian Bottiglieri and Carl Michael Lindner were cast as the Bergman's precocious five-year-old sons.

The pilot was shot, but again the powers that be tossed a flag on the play. Testing had shown the audience was put off by the perceived age difference between Gene and Jennifer Grey. So, yet a third pilot was shot with Daytime Emmy award-winning actress Hilary Bailey Smith replacing Grey in the role of Annie.

The only snag was that Hilary was under contract to ABC in New York. Warner's worked out an agreement whereby we would share Hilary with her hit ABC daytime soap *One Life to Live.* Hilary would shoot in New York on Mondays and Tuesdays, then jet to L.A. Tuesday night to rehearse and shoot *Wilder* on Wednesdays, Thursdays, and Fridays. She would return to New York on Saturday and repeat the entire process the following week.

Barnet would be sole executive producer and direct every episode, a *big* plus for the show. By this time Barnet and I had become the top pilot directing and producing duo on the Warner Bros. lot. But the network, in their infinite wisdom, determined Lee did not have the requisite skills to run a writer's room. Barnet would have to bring in writers who would partner with him.

Lee could be a co-executive producer. Despite the demotion, Lee still received the valuable "created by" credit, so he would be rewarded financially if the show was a hit. Warner's brought writer Ruth Bennett in to partner with Barnet, along with Tom Anderson from *Cheers*. They hired a staff of journeymen and promising but inexperienced young writers.

The writer's room on a situation comedy show usually starts about eight weeks prior to the first taping. Now Barnet is a terrific director, and I was expecting him to be a terrific executive producer too. But he disappointed me, and by doing so disappointed Lee and Gene as well.. On the day the writers room opened, he announced he was leaving for a seven-week vacation with the family to the Hampton's.

I expressed my concerns, which he promptly dismissed.

"We will be fine. Lee will be here to watch them."

This ain't good, I thought.

Barnet had already let the studio and the network cut off Lee's balls. I knew this was a harbinger of bad things to come.

In the interim, Gene Wilder was delightful but quiet and non-intrusive. How many talk shows have you ever seen Gene appear on? None. Zero. He was a comedic actor not a raconteur or a haha funny man.

He did make minimal requests to production. For example, he wanted to sing the theme song, "You Brought a New Kind of Love to Me," a song made famous when Chico and Harpo Marx mimed singer Maurice Chevalier's hit record in the 1931 Marx Brothers' classic *Monkey Business*. We quickly obtained the rights to the tune.

Gene was also a painter of note and asked if several of his paintings could hang on the set. We happily accommodated both of those simple requests. One of these paintings now proudly hangs in my office, thanks to a donation of mine to Gilda's Club. Other than that, unsurprisingly, Gene trusted Barnet and his writing crew. He had no reason not to.

Gene and I got to know and confide in each other during that pre-production period.

While Barnet whiled away his days on the beach in the Hamptons, the writers' room was a mess. Lee had no say in any of the scripts. With no back-end points, Ruth and Tom really didn't have any vested interest in the show. Al Gore had not yet "invented the internet", so Barnet tried to stay involved by phone. That enabled Ruth, the writing staff's spokesperson, to paint a prettier picture then the end product would ultimately reveal.

Barnet returned to L.A. less than a week before the actual table read to assemble the cast for a pre-table read at Barnet's house. It was the first time they would see the script, and the first time the writers would hear their words spoken.

The writers had changed Lee's script completely. Gene was aghast.

When the pre-table concluded, Gene pulled me and Barnet aside. "This is terrible. I am not reading this script tomorrow."

Good for him.

Barnet tried to talk Gene out of it, telling him it wasn't in the best interest of the show.

Gene stood firm, saying it wasn't in his best interest to move forward with such a lousy script. We immediately got the studio on the phone. They agreed we should substitute scripts in an attempt to save face. We would read our second episode then the pilot. The episode involved Gene's niece, Katy, having a pen pal in jail. Gene would visit the prison to ask the inmate to stop writing to her. I had anticipated a problem but kept my mouth shut. Why write about a secondary character so soon? And, okay, I get the *Silver Streak* reference to the jail, but that reference was benign at best and certainly didn't warrant the confusion an added character would cause.

The studio in turn got the network on the phone, and the table read was pushed ahead one day to allow the writers to put a little more "polish" on the script.

There wasn't enough polish in the world for this turd either. Of course, the Monday morning rewrite wasn't any better. The show went on an unscheduled hiatus for a week, an appalling way to start a series.

Who the heck was in charge here?

With Barnet back, the show finally started taking a little form. Ruth had gradually seized the show from Tom and, truthfully, wasn't packing the gear to run the writers' room. She took every note from everyone. Too many chefs make for a sloppy smorgasbord, so naturally show nights were a chaotic mess.

We would bring an audience of about 250 people to see each show. The audience threw Gene for a loop.

"Why are they here?" Gene whispered to me.

"The network thinks the energy from the audience makes the show funnier."

He responded humbly in classic Gene Wilder understatement, "Gee, I have been known to make some pretty funny movies without an audience."

Gene had me there.

The warm-up comic also threw Gene. As the writers were frantically rewriting humorless material that still wouldn't work, the actors desperately tried to memorize their lines. Just get the words in the right order. "The hell with the subtext" became the mantra. The audience found themselves laughing louder at the warm-up jokes than they were the actual script.

Again, chaos.

By episode two, we had brought in a band, a quartet outfitted in tuxedos to play dance music. The writers christened them the Berkowitz Bar Mitzvah Band, but they were actually quite good if not a little out of place. Gene was delighted with the band. When I told Gene what the writers had christened the band, he lit up, "What do you know? They finally wrote something funny!"

In years of observing both casts and audiences, I have noticed they only have a maximum two-and-a-half-hour attention span. Anything after that has diminishing returns.

Some nights with all the rewrites, our people were there for nearly five hours. By 11 p.m. Friday night, we would be down to about 100 or so lingerers. The poor warm-up comic would be juggling and riding a unicycle in an attempt to keep everyone awake. I would bring Gene a small snifter of Polish potato vodka to help carry him to the finish line.

I have to say, Gene and the cast, which also included Gregory Itzin and Jake Weber, were, week in and week out, pure delights to work with. I also must mention to Barnet's credit, each episode did improve by show night and cut together really well.

One Friday show night, as was customary, the network was asking for next week's script. Ruth Bennett intended to cancel Monday's table read because the writers had only written one act of the next episode. The network and the studio suits would have none of it.

Warner Bros. demanded the writers work all weekend. Deliver a script or don't bother to show up for work Monday morning was the mandate. Any other competent executive producer would have known to work through the weekend without having to be asked, not Ruth. To protect their jobs, the writers showed up for work on Monday with a completed script.

About two weeks later, they brought in Chris Thompson, a noted writing savant as a consultant. Chris took a quick look at the chaos in the writers' room and, after one week, bolted like a metal rabbit at a greyhound track.

Out of ideas, the network demanded something be done.

So, what did they do?

They fired Lee Kalcheim, the one guy crucial to the process. The one guy who had been neutralized and marginalized by studio and network politics. Think what you want about Lee, but Barnet had a second chance here to make a stand on Lee's behalf and again failed to step up. Barnet was supposed to be our leader. The fact that he didn't support Lee was bullshit.

We had rocker Alice Cooper guest star on an episode, and the second Mrs. Donald Trump, Marla Maples, appear on another. Gene preferred really funny supporting guests, such as recurring actress Debra Mooney, who had evolved into the perfect foil for Gene in the way that Margaret Dumont served Groucho Marx.

"Why are we having such big-name guest stars?" Gene would lament.

"The network is looking for stunts for the show," I said.

"Gee, I thought I was the stunt!"

Score another one for Gene.

To help the struggling Bennett, we finally brought in Jonathan Prince, who became sort of a voice to run the writing room. From that point on, the scripts were better. With Jonathan steering the writing and with Barnet's direction, we started to hit our stride.

But it was too late.

We actually got picked up for extra episodes, but the last four shows never aired. If they did air, NBC buried them so early in the morning that we became the lead-in for *Sunrise Sermonette*.

Gene had learned his lesson and was rarely seen on series television again, except a notable 2002 appearance on *Will and Grace,* for which he was awarded an Emmy. His movie masterpieces, however, will live on forever.

Barnet and Lee made up, and Barnet and I have worked together many times since, most recently on *Murphy Brown* in November 2018.

As for Lee, he and Julia are doing well. The two boys are borderline geniuses. Both have master's degrees and are pursuing their doctorates.

Ruth Bennett? She's missing in action. I guess the old adage is true. "All stains do come clean in the final wash."

This painting by Gene hangs in my office. (Mitchell Haddad Photography)

Gene Wilder was a gentleman on and off the set. (PF Collection)

"REMEMBER THE GAL WHO GAVE UP? NOBODY ELSE DOES EITHER."

– Author unknown

Chapter 13

THE LITTLE ENGINE
THAT COULD

"No high school in the nation had more Division 1 signees for girls' soccer than Flintridge Sacred Heart."—Eric Sondheimer, *L.A. Times*, February 3, 2012

We did it.

Having won what one coach called, "the most rigorous high school girls soccer tournament anywhere in the nation," we were finally the CIF Division 1 Champions, bringing with it the number one ranking in the land. But it wasn't easy for this small Catholic girl's school tucked off atop a hill overlooking the Rose Bowl in La Canada, California.

It was anything but easy.

The seeds for the 1–0 win over mighty San Clemente High School had been sown in 1995 when a twenty-six-year old teacher took over as soccer coach. Kathy Desmond was more than qualified to take the head coaching reins at Flintridge Sacred Heart Academy (FSHA). She had been a great player at Sonoma State University, leading them to the D-2 national finals in her senior season.

Still, I thought to myself maybe she could use a little help.

I was doing it for selfish reasons. Our only daughter Erin had enrolled at FSHA in 1998. I wanted to steal two hours a day with her on the soccer field. I had played goalkeeper in college in the '70s and coached a little in the early '90s.

When I approached Kathy to help her with coaching, she grudgingly said fine.

"I just thought he was another pain in the neck parent," Kathy said. "Little did I know." (Hmmm read that any way you want).

When I took on my co-head coaching duties, I was producing *Suddenly Susan* and *For Your Love*. It would be a delicate balancing act not to let Warner Bros. know I was coaching. They would have frowned upon it. Of course, I would have copped to it immediately if anyone asked.

Fortunately, no one asked.

Every day, I would drop off Erin for school, work through lunch until 2:30 p.m., and then hustle to the field to coach until 4:45. Since I was producing two shows, each had assumed I was at the other one's stage. Using my two-seater for a locker room, I'd race ten miles back to the studio and work until 7:30.

FSHA had a pretty good Division 4 team in 1998–99. The school was blessed with possibly the best high school player I had ever seen anywhere, Jessica Reyes. She went on to play college soccer, making Regional All-American twice at Colorado College her freshman and sophomore years. Colorado College Head Coach Greg Ryan booted her off the team before her junior year for disciplinary reasons. I ran into Greg years later after he had been named head coach for the US Women's National Team.

He agreed with my assessment of Jessica's talents. What a shame. She would have been a terrific addition to the US Women's National Team and a worthy successor to Mia Hamm. To Jessica's credit, she used that disappointment to turn her life around. With soccer no longer available, she channeled that competitiveness to make her mark in the business world, where she thrives today.

When Erin graduated and moved on to the University of Kentucky, I probably would have left FSHA had it not been for one game. The Chaminade game during the first week of January 1999 just stuck in my craw.

After eight games of non-league competition, our first league contest was played on Chaminade's home field. We were coming off a three-week holiday layoff, but the perennial powerhouse had played through the holiday break. We were no match for them. They didn't just beat us. They embarrassed us 9–0. I vowed right then and there, no matter how long it took, a humiliation like that would never be inflicted on our girls again. Nor would we ever demean an opponent.

My first step toward that resolve took place that very night. Our girls stayed after the game, and while their shocked parents watched from the stands, Kathy and I made them run sprints until they almost puked. We never took the holidays off again.

That year we had six freshmen make the varsity team. One who didn't was a little girl named Jessica Hanson. After we had played several games, Erin asked me over dinner who I thought was the best freshman we had. I answered. She said no. This went back and forth several times. Each time that I shot out a name, Erin gave the same answer.

Finally, I lifted an exasperated eyebrow. "Who then?"

The corner of her mouth quirked upwards. "Hanson," she said.

The following day when I told Kathy, we agreed to take another look at Jessica. What we saw was a skinny, little blonde girl, very quick, who measured 5'3." She barely weighed 100 pounds soaking wet, but 80 of those pounds were sheer heart. We can justify our earlier decision by saying we didn't think that Jessica wanted to play with her sister, who was a senior on the varsity team, but that would be revisionist history. The truth is we made a mistake.

A huge mistake.

Erin was right. There was no measuring her heart. We moved Jessica up to the varsity midway through her freshman year, and by her junior season, she was the Area Player of the Year. In her senior year, she had grown to 5'8", and her body had matured. She was still as quick as a jackrabbit, but now she could play physical as well.

She committed to play Division 1 soccer for Kit Vela at the University of New Mexico. In a last-minute change of heart, she chose to attend Loyola Marymount University in Los Angeles. She wanted to be closer to home so that her parents could watch her play.

In her very first game at LMU, Jessica scored the only goal in an overtime triumph versus San Jose State. After the game, she tossed me a mini game ball and with a shit-eating grin said, "Not good enough as a freshman at Sacred Heart, eh?"

The Pace family were very close with the Hanson's. Jessica was Erin's best friend. Jessica's dad, Kelly, had been in a severe car accident several years earlier and could no longer work as an accountant in the firm he had founded. He had only recently resumed driving.

"Can you get him out of the house?" his wife, Bindy, pleaded. "He will do anything."

I went to my assistant director, Rosario, and we hired him as a factory worker extra on *George Lopez*. He would work two days a week with the understanding that he was not to tell anyone how he knew me in the unlikely event anyone even asked.

That said, I was no longer working two shows. I was now producing only one, and my relationship with George was such that there were no secrets between us. I needed to get his permission for me to continue to coach. There is no doubt in my mind that if George had said no, I would have quit coaching in 2002.

Waving his hand like the Godfather, George gave me the okay to continue. It would be our loosely kept secret from that point on.

I did use the studio name, however, for the benefit of our girls. We were starting to attract higher-quality players. First, Lauren Johnson came, followed by Hannah Hand, Lauren Bustos, Carly Crowder, and a host of really good players who were also excellent students. They all wanted to play in college.

Prior to my arrival, no graduate from FSHA had ever played college soccer. That was a shame because Kelly Sinner was a great player for Kathy in earlier years. She went to Vanderbilt and didn't play soccer but knew the minute she got on campus that she had made a mistake. By then, it was too late for Kelly. I stepped in to make sure that wouldn't happen again, becoming a vocal advocate for our girls.

How?

I relentlessly called coaches at college after college across the country. They invariably wouldn't take my calls, but I would leave a message to return my call at "Warner Bros. Studio offices in Burbank." I deliberately left out the reason why they should call.

Their curiosity piqued, they couldn't dial quickly enough. Once they called, I had them. My dad used to say about me, "If bullshit was music, you would be the whole brass band." I don't know if that is 100 percent true, but I am a public relations guy. Pushing our players on the phone came easily to me.

Of course, the coach would have to see the player in action, but Kathy and I had fine players. We would take our chances when the girls showed their wares on the field.

A college recruiter calculates several factors into their decision. Most are objective. First and foremost are the high school grades. Second are the SAT or ACT scores. Third are the family finances. (How much money are they willing to spend?) Most schools don't give full scholarships. Next is geography. The farther from home one is willing to travel, the more expansive the opportunities.

The only subjective factor is if the coach thinks the girl can play. We have no control over that one.

More than 1,000 schools play college soccer at the NCAA, NAIA, or JUCO levels, 350 of them play NCAA Division 1 soccer. Many of the top academic schools like Williams, Swarthmore, and Johns Hopkins play Division 3. Our task was to find a coach who thought one of our girls could play. If we found two coaches, even better.

Obviously, the more girls we placed in college, the more girls would be attracted to our private high school.

My public relations background also helped me schmooze the local newspapers and develop really strong relationships. Boy, did that pay off. When it was time for the All-Area selections, and later All-State and All-America, the media members had seen our players in high-profile matches and remembered them.

In 2004, my friend Aleks Mihailovic called from Chicago. He asked me to assist him in coaching the Midwest Select team in Minnesota. Aleks, a former pro player, is the finest soccer mind I know, and it was an honor to be asked. His four-year-old son, Djordje, tagged along. Now a twenty-year-old member of the US Men's National Team, Djordje is also the starting center midfielder on the Chicago Fire.

As it turns out, Jessica Hanson would play on the western Region 4 select team. In the tournament, the four regions would compete, and the eighteen players deemed the four teams' finest players would be chosen to play on the US national Select Team, where Aleks would be a coach. That US Select team would go on to play Australia's national team two days later in the Aussies' final tune-up before the World Cup.

Our Region 2 team had an outstanding twenty-one-year-old player, the captain of the University of Miami squad, Jenna Johnson. On the way to our second game, Jenna approached me on the team bus.

"You're a producer?" she asked.

I don't know how she knew. It wasn't relevant, so I had not mentioned it. Maybe Aleks let it slip? But like I said above, she was one hell of a player.

"I am a film major," Jenna said. "Miami requires an internship for graduation as part of my core curriculum. I was wondering if you could help."

I told her that Warner Bros. had a very strict policy on interns. We could only consider her if she was working for school credit and then for an entire semester. There would be no pay, and we had to work off a syllabus provided by her teachers to make sure we were fulfilling all her school requirements.

Jenna said she could get that material from the university and gave it to me before we left Minnesota. We hired Jenna with two caveats.

One, she had to be at the studio promptly by 8:30 a.m. on January 3, 2005. There would be a drive-on pass waiting for her at the security gate. If she was one minute late, the guard would be instructed to revoke the pass and tell Jenna her internship offer had been rescinded.

Two, she had to assist Kathy and me at Sacred Heart with our high school coaching. She agreed. In the following four months she never once called for instructions or directions. Good thing that I was at the studio early on January 3. She showed up at 7:30 a.m.

Jenna made the US national Select Team. I was delighted watching her in the starting lineup, playing for her nation, proudly wearing the stars and stripes as the band blared our national anthem. Jessica failed to make that year's squad, but she would eventually be given another shot in 2005.

Meanwhile back at FSHA, we were coming into our own. We were winning games, just not the big ones. We kept working. Kathy and I had developed a nice coaching rapport. One newspaper described us like this: "Kathy was the quiet one in the hoodie and shorts. Frank was the frenzy in dress shoes and slacks." That was until Kathy got angry. That's when the girls knew they had better get their acts together.

The following summer, Jessica was invited back to the US national Select Team tryout camp. This time she was selected to the team that would travel to Mexico to play in July. Like Jenna before her, she, too, had the opportunity to wear the stars and stripes of this great nation. Each girl said it was the proudest moment of their soccer lives. Mine too.

In early August, I had taken the morning off to play nine holes with George Lopez at Lakeside Golf Club. It was a hiatus week, and I had forgotten to take my phone. When I entered the office, it was as solemn as a confessional. I knew something was wrong.

"What is it?" I asked.

Silence.

"Tell me it's not Erin?" I pleaded.

Jenna, who had now been hired as full-time staff, lowered her head. Sadness clouded the features of everyone in the room. She muttered two devastating words, "It's Hanson."

On her way to Lake Havasu for one last vacation before the start of her senior season at LMU, the inconceivable had happened. Along with her dad, her fiancé, and another passenger, Jessica had been killed in a car crash.

The accident took place some 350 miles from L.A., but ironically only a few miles from the site of the crash that had almost taken her dad's life years before. The cause of both crashes was eerily the same. The intense 120-degree desert heat had caused the overheated tires to explode.

Everybody in our community was devastated.

How could a person be so alive one minute and the next minute be gone? Jenna helped me get through all the logistics and prepare for the funeral mass. The Holy Family Church in South Pasadena was jammed with Jessica's teammates from Sacred Heart and Loyola, plus a multitude of grieving friends the Hanson's had made over the years.

I never could have gotten through it without my wife, Karen, my daughter Erin, and the exceptional Jenna.

Four months later, the weight of the world got considerably heavier. Not satisfied with Jessica, the angel of death flew down to snuff out yet another young life full of remarkable promise.

While training for the L.A. Marathon, Jenna Johnson collapsed dead on the pavement. She never had a chance. The autopsy showed a congenital heart defect, one that couldn't be diagnosed by the many physicals she had undergone in her athletic career.

That Friday before Jenna's death, we had defeated our local rival Flintridge Prep. I will never forget waving goodbye to Jenna as she walked up the hill from the field to her car and saying, "See you Monday."

"Monday" never came.

That Sunday, I had been given the terrible task of identifying Jenna's body. Hours later, Kathy and I had to quickly assemble all the girls and their parents to tell them the news of Jenna's passing. My PR skills couldn't help me now. There was no sugarcoating the facts. Jenna had tragically passed away.

FSHA was reeling. Two remarkably beloved and gifted young spirits snuffed and gone within four months. Just like that. The other girls had only known Jessica through alumni games. Not the way Kathy and I had. When their assistant coach Jenna was taken, I could see the question marks on their young faces as though they were daring Kathy and me to explain how this horrible tragedy could have happened.

Everyone was devastated.

It would be hard to get them back on task. Our girls showed their great character by playing through the heartbreak. We struggled through our next couple of games, yet we still won and somehow were able to advance to the finals of a Christmas Tournament against Flintridge Prep yet again.

Mimi Roukoz scored the only goal of the game, and we squeaked out a 1–0 win. After the game, the girls presented Jenna's parents, who had come out from Chicago to accompany the body home, with the Most Valuable Player Award. Despite the win, there wasn't much joy in the players' faces that day.

The staff of *George Lopez* was also shocked. Remember, only a few months before, the crew had lost Kelly Hanson. Jenna had integrated herself into the fabric of the show and became a vital part of our production team. I swear she was on the fast track to becoming a producer. George paid all the expenses for Jenna's funeral, including transporting the body back to Chicago.

That March we honored Jenna by running a relay and finishing the very marathon she had been training for. George would run the final mile with Jenna's still-grieving mom. If life was ever a movie, this was one of those times.

While we kept winning on the field, FSHA had entered an era of ill fortune off the field. Between 2002 and 2009, we not only lost Jessica and Jenna but also, incredibly enough, six of the team fathers passed away. The grief was constant and at times unbearable. When would it end? I became almost obsessed with winning—if only for everyone who had taken our program so far.

We won fourteen games in 2007 but our quest for the league title still fell short. For one reason or another, 2008 found us sliding back to fourth place, even missing the playoffs. Still, I felt that 2009 could be our year. A solid batch of really good, cocky freshman had enrolled in school, and we had a terrific core of seniors to hold the freshman in check. We won sixteen games and captured our long awaited first league title 1–0 on a late goal by Sinead Fleming.

And who did we beat in that championship game?

Not only did we beat our rival school Chaminade, we beat them on their home turf. After years that had seemed like decades, satisfaction was ours.

As delighted as I was for the girls, the victory's memory will always be bittersweet. I wasn't able to witness the Chaminade game because my cherished mom had passed. I had flown back east for her funeral.

There was no texting then, nor much of an internet to speak of. Hours after we laid my mom to rest and the events of the day was over, I had the chance to check my voicemail messages. Our entire team was yelling into the phone, "We won! We won!" Whether it was for my mom or for the girls or probably for a little of both, on the dreadful day we buried my mom, there alone sitting in my boyhood bedroom, overcome with emotion, I broke down and cried like a baby.

We lost to eventual champions Saugus High School in the CIF playoff 1–0. The next season we failed to advance past the D-2 semifinals, being eliminated on penalty kicks by Beckman High School, who then lost to our league rivals Harvard Westlake, the eventual champions. Harvard Westlake had a record of 8-1-1 in league play—with their only loss and tie coming to us.

We were undefeated in league play. We had a 7-0-3 record, but our three ties placed us one point behind Harvard Westlake in second place. When we made it to the semifinals of the CIF, we had qualified for the California State Regional Tournament. In the state tournament, teams are grouped by the size of their schools. With only 395 girls, we were placed in D-3. We fell behind 1–0 in the championship game to San Diego's Francis Parker High but came back to win 2–1 and capture our first state title.

As good as the victory felt—and it felt really good—we still had some unfinished business. Based on our finish in 2010, we were elevated to Division 1 the following season. We were more than up for the challenge. Kathy and I even printed "Unfinished Business" warm-up shirts.

We had not officially lost in the calendar year 2010, and we were ready. (Note: Failing to advance on penalty kicks are counted as ties on your record.)

Led by Katie Johnson and Kayla Mills, who would later pair up again in college to lead USC to an NCAA title, and Breeana Koemans, our high-scoring offense combined with our lockdown defense to stretch our unbeaten streak to thirty-six games before we finally lost to Harvard Westlake.

We came back from that defeat to win the league and advance to the CIF D-1 playoffs. The playoffs are usually skewed in favor of the powerful Orange County teams. This year would be no different. In addition, we would still have to get through league foe Harvard Westlake lurking on the other side of the draw.

We rolled through the first game and advanced through the second on penalty kicks. We won the third game 3–1 but lost our starting goalkeeper in the final seconds to a broken hand. She would miss the remainder of the playoffs.

Harvard Westlake was knocked out of the tournament early, giving us one less bridge to cross, but we still had a particularly tough road to bear.

We squeezed through the semifinals on our opponent's home field when Alyssa Conti booted home the only goal of the game in overtime. Then we won another 1–0 cliffhanger over San Clemente, on a goal in the sixty-seventh minute by Krista Meaglia in front of a massive crowd in the finals.

Our little school of 395 girls had scaled the mountaintop and overcome adversity by beating the top three schools in the national ratings. When we beat one, the other took over the number one spot, and so on and so on, until finally, there was no one left to beat.

At last, our little engine had climbed Everest. We were indisputably and gloriously number 1 in the country.

If a picture could say more than 1,000 words, our championship shot would be the *War and Peace* of photographs. Look at the unbridled joy on the girls' faces as their index fingers point skyward.

It is terrific.

Also notice that I am holding a patch, which I carried in my pocket throughout the entire tournament. It is a patch we wore on our shirts in 2005 to commemorate the passing of Jessica Hanson. I wanted her to share this experience too.

After the game, one of the parents, Dennis Johnson, who had two daughters play for us from 2006 through 2012, asked me what gave me more satisfaction, being nominated for an Emmy or winning a CIF championship.

The answer came easy. Winning the CIF title because that was objective. It was all about the girls. They proved they were the best. In the 2010 and 2011 seasons, all told our record was 45-3-5. The weekly polls had us ranked number one in the nation five times over a three-year span, including pre-season number 1 in 2012.

Not bad.

Kathy left the program after the 2012 season but stayed on at the school, where she is now the academic dean. I remained on to help transition the new coach for the following season. I still go back every year to present the Jessica Hanson Award to the Most Valuable Player and the Jenna Johnson Award to the Most Improved Player. To this day, their photos are displayed proudly in the school gym. Their legacies will never die.

From schools like Notre Dame to MIT to Northwestern to Johns Hopkins, we have placed more than sixty-five players on college rosters nationwide. FSHA has produced lawyers, doctors, financial planners, teachers, and just all-around really solid kids. I always said, "We don't coach them for four years; we coach them for a lifetime." And if I ever need a lawyer or a doctor, well, that is just an added benefit.

No. Not too bad.

We won on the scoreboard as our kids are winning in the game of life. I will close this chapter with the same words that I used to close both Jessica and Jenna's eulogies in 2005:

"Death comes to us all, but great achievements build monuments which shall endure until the sun grows cold. Fulfill your potential, so when we meet up again, we can get that pat on the back and hear the words 'well done.'"

Victorious #1 team in the nation. Notice the patch in my left hand to honor the late Jessica Hanson, #4. (Courtesy of Flintridge Sacred Heart)

Daughter Erin, my reason for getting into coaching. (Courtesy Flintridge Sacred Heart)

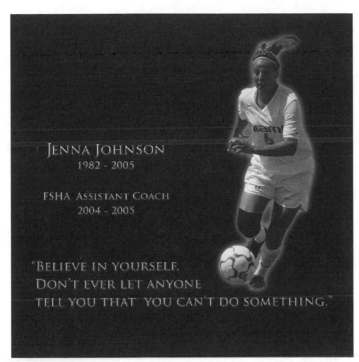

Jenna Johnson's photo sits aside Jess Hanson's at FSHA. We lost both girls within five months. (Courtesy of Matt Copping)

With Jessica Hanson at US Select Camp in Minnesota. (Courtesy of Aleks Mihailovic)

"MY NIECE WAS IN THE GLASS MENAGERIE. THEY USED TUPPERWARE."

– *Cathy Ladman*

Chapter 14

THE DISNEY YEARS

In 2009, I was in a bit of a slump. In the two years prior, I had produced a movie, a documentary, and an HBO special for George Lopez. Although satisfying, it wasn't the steady series work I was used to. I wasn't accustomed to searching for my next job.

During lunch with Armen Keteyian in Manhattan, my cell phone rang. It was the writer Billy Van Zandt.

My ears perked up.

"Do you want to do a pilot for Disney?"

"Yeah. Sure," I said.

"Well, call me when you get home."

Disney wasn't offering my usual salary but would guarantee a minimum of twenty-two to twenty-eight episodes per year. Studios always pay producers, directors, writers, and actors by the episode. With the current television landscape changing toward fewer episodes per season, the offer was appealing. I thrive on the action, anyway.

Also did I mention I was in a bit of a slump?

The results of that call took up the next eight years of my life, allowing me to work with child stars Zendaya, Bella Thorne, Sabrina Carpenter, and Rowan Blanchard, among others. The hours were nice too. Due to child labor laws, children can't work more than nine-and-a-half hours a day, and three of those hours must be spent in show-provided classrooms. On shows without kids, I have often worked twelve to fourteen hours a day. During those eight years, I shared multiple Emmy nominations but received plenty of bumps and bruises for my efforts.

We shot Billy Van Zandt and Jane Milmore's pilot, *Jack and Janet Save the Planet,* on the same stage that Al Jolson had filmed the first talkie, *The Jazz Singer*, in 1927. Billy and Jane's pilot never went to series, but Disney production executive Amanda Ramey and her boss Susette Hsiung thought enough of me to offer another project, *Shake It Up*, before *Jack and Janet* had even wrapped.

They asked if I knew Chris Thompson.

Did I know Chris Thompson?

Chris Thompson was one of the most brilliant creative minds to come out of the last quarter of the twentieth century. The only catch was that Chris was addicted to drugs and alcohol, lots and lots of drugs and alcohol. Everybody in our industry knew Chris's problems, but he was still getting jobs.

Like I said, Chris was brilliant. He had discovered Tom Hanks and Peter Scolari and cast them in a little show he had created called *Bosom Buddies*. But like I also said, Chris was known to enter a writers' room, lay down lines of coke, and snort them with a quart of vodka as a chaser. Chris and I had met on the show *Something Wilder*. He had come in as a creative consultant in mid-season. In less than a week, he had assessed the writing staff as hopeless and was gone. Still, we hit it off.

He went on to create a load of shows, including *The Naked Truth* starring Tea Leoni. Married with a couple of kids, Chris ended up leaving his wife for Tea. They moved in together and carried on a torrid love affair for a year-and-a-half or so. I would often see Chris, a terrific golfer, and Tea, pretty good at swinging the sticks herself, at Lakeside Golf Club, which is located almost catty-corner from Warner Bros. Studios. Clean cut and cordial, Chris, who was a member, looked and dressed like a golf pro.

Hoping I would produce *Shake It Up*, Susette and Amanda asked me to meet with Chris, which was a bit surprising considering his history. Chris was obviously not the logical choice for a Disney Channel kids' show, but people change, I suppose. If the Disney Channel was fine with Chris, so was I.

At that meeting, I almost didn't recognize Chris.

Wearing a T-shirt and blue jeans, he was heavily tattooed, with a scruffy goatee and long straggly hair. He was showing the ravishes of time and alcohol, but still we greeted each other warmly. Before the waitress had even brought us a menu, he asked, "So, are we going to do this?"

I had read the script, as I always do before I take a meeting, but I was still surprised by the directness of his question.

"That's not up to me," I cracked. "You're the boss, remember?"

"Then let's do it," he smiled.

Although packaged differently, he was the same warm and friendly Chris whom I had remembered, and the talent hadn't faded. He had written a terrific pilot.

We cast a young mixed-race girl from Oakland, California— Zendaya Coleman—to play Rocky, and a lithe, redheaded, waiflike Bella Thorne from Miami to play Cece. The show had two Chicago high school students aspiring to be dancers. Each show featured *big* dance numbers in which Zendaya and Bella were surrounded by an equally talented cast.

Disney creatives told us Zendaya would be the better dancer and Bella the better actress. With his usual foresight, Chris said that was complete bullshit. Both girls were major talents on their way to bigger and better things.

The pilot was a huge hit.

Within seven months, we were shooting the first of three seasons. Rob Lotterstein, who I had worked with previously on *Suddenly Susan,* was hired to collaborate with Chris. As much as they wanted Chris's genius, Disney was afraid he would self-destruct, so Rob was their insurance policy.

Chris immediately brought in the director Joel Zwick, whom he had worked with on the *Bosom Buddies* pilot. Joel, who had dated singer-songwriter Carole King when they were teenagers and ran track with Bernie Sanders in the same Brooklyn, New York high school, was a comedy veteran going back to *Laverne and Shirley* and *Family Matters.* Joel had threatened retirement, but Chris—in another stroke of genius—talked him out of it. Nearing seventy, the director exuded energy and was a perfect match for our high-powered teenaged cast.

Chris adored the cast, especially Zendaya, but he took particular interest in Bella. Whereas Zendaya had two secure parents in a long-term marriage, Bella's dad had died in a motorcycle accident when she was only eight years old, leaving her overmatched young mother with four kids to raise. It was often too much. Chris sensed Bella's emotional isolation and worked hard to be the kind father like figure her life was missing. I sensed Bella appreciated Chris's attention.

Other than the needless drama created by their agents—who would be billed first on the call sheets for example—we never had any problems on stage. (We ended up alternating Zendaya and Bella in the number 1 position for a half season each).

Backstage was another story.

Still haunted by his demons, Chris was fired by Disney after that first season. Bella's father figure was taken away, and it hurt her—but not as much as it hurt Chris. Chris died of a reported heart attack in 2015. Upon his death Bella tweeted, "You were like a Dad to me at an early age and protected me through many years. I will love and miss you always."

Chris Thompson finally found the peace in death that his brilliant mind wouldn't allow him in life.

With Rob Lotterstein now in sole charge of the show, it was smooth sailing from there on in. Zendaya and Bella both lived up to their enormous potential as actors and dancers, and the entire cast was superb. I would work with any of them again in a minute.

The public absolutely loved *Shake it Up*. Each week, an assortment of high-profile guests and their children arranged to visit the set. One week, our company was extra special.

Erika Williams is a graduate of Stanford and Yale Law schools and she was one of Kobe Bryant's agents. I had known Erika since her high school days as an outstanding soccer player.

One day she called to ask if Kobe, his wife Vanessa, and two daughters, Natalia and Gigi, could visit.

"The girls adore Zendaya and Bella," she gushed.

"We would love that," I said.

We kept that conversation between Erika and me quiet right up until the day Kobe's limo pulled up outside Stage 3 at the L.A. Center Studios. Watching the cast work through their dance steps, Kobe, Vanessa, and his girls were in awe—almost as much as Zendaya, Bella, and the rest of the cast and crew were in awe of them.

During a break in the action, I told Kobe of my great friendship with Artis Gilmore. His eyes got as wide as bicycle rims.

"I have known Artis since I was eight years old," Kobe said. "He and my dad played basketball in Italy for a year. Artis and I used to shoot baskets together before practice and games. He was wonderful to me."

"Would you like me to get Artis on the phone?" I asked.

"That would be great," Kobe said.

Artis was delighted. He and Kobe greeted each other in Italian then proceeded to laugh and tell stories for ten minutes or so.

"That made my day," Kobe said, handing me back the phone.

The friendships between the Bryant's and the girls, especially Zendaya, flourished from that day on. Zendaya even spent New Year's Eve 2020 at the Bryant home in Newport Beach. That was only twenty-five days before the fatal helicopter crash that took Kobe and Gianna.

Zendaya has gone on to become a one-name superstar, so much so that no one even knows her last name. Bella, God love her, has made an impression in her own right as an actress, singer, and best-selling author.

For their next series, Disney execs Susette and Amanda wanted me again. *Girl Meets World* was conceived as a continuation of ABC's '90's megahit *Boy Meets World. Girl Meets World* would return Ben Savage and Danielle Fishel to their roles as Cory Mathews and Topanga, now as man and wife, bringing up two kids of their own in New York City.

Then the good Lord threw me a knuckleball.

In January 2013, I suffered a dissected carotid artery, which caused a massive stroke, forcing me to miss four to five weeks of work. I was sure my career was toast. Yet Susette, Amanda, and the Disney Studios supported me completely. To this day, I am eternally grateful. When I returned, I only worked part-time for the season's final two episodes. Bella, Zendaya, the cast, and the writers were great about it. Looking past my limitations, we wrapped in mid-March.

In May, Disney wanted me to meet with *Girl's* executive producer and creator, Michael Jacobs. Susette, Amanda, and I all agreed that Michael didn't need to know about the stroke. Why? Remember George Lopez's quote about the tomato can? Now, I was the dented tomato can.

The show was slated to start production in August with a reshoot of the original pilot, which had been taped while we were wrapping *Shake It Up.* By now, I was maybe three quarters back—still not in tip-top shape.

If I could get through this meeting with Michael, I was sure I would be back to almost full strength by July. I was apprehensive before the meeting and got even more so when Michael walked in with his "Three

Wise Men": Jeff Menell, Matt Nelson, and Mark Blutman, all of whom had worked with him as writers on *Boy Meets World*.

I needn't have worried. When I said hello, Michael looked at my résumé, saw Rod Carew's name, and spoke baseball nonstop for twenty minutes. No one else in the room got in a word. I got the job. It foreshadowed things to come.

A talented and interesting man, Michael was a dominant figure in television comedy in the '80s and '90s. He created not only the iconic hit *Boy Meets World* but also long-running successes *Dinosaurs, My Two Dads*, and *Charles in Charge*. Jacobs, however, had a reputation as a difficult man to work for. When paired with me, this was a recipe ripe for disaster. I don't suffer fools easily.

Michael and I grew to respect each other, and I even have to admit a grudging fondness for the man. That said, at times I often found Michael to be a narcissist, an egomaniac, a misogynist, and a bully who created a crisis just so he could swoop in and say he had fixed the problem. All of that and yet he is a devoutly religious man. (Sounds like a lot of current-day politicians).

Michael hadn't had a hit show since *Boy Meets World* went off the air in 2000. Even though he had been writing in Florida, this show was maybe his last chance to return to the prominence he had enjoyed at the end of the twentieth century.

Our cast wasn't at all like *Shake It Up's*. The two stars were Rowan Blanchard and Sabrina Carpenter. Rowan was brought up in a "Hollywood family" and was Hollywood through and through. Her dad was a director, and her mom was also in show business, as were her younger sister and brother. Sabrina, an aspiring singer, was more grounded.

Except for Sabrina and Peyton Meyers, a good-looking baseball player turned actor from Las Vegas, the rest of the cast was similar to Rowan. All of them actively courted stardom. While the *Shake It Up* cast were fun-loving, the *Girl Meets World* kids were mischievous. While the *Shake It Up* kids were courteous and respectful to their elders, the *Girl Meets World* kids were at times incorrigible. While the *Shake It Up* kids never brought their cellphones on stage, the *Girl Meets World* kids were tied to theirs.

The legacy cast noticed the differences too. The show's star, Ben Savage, said to me, "When we did the original, we didn't have social media. It took a year before we noticed how popular we were getting. We respected our teachers. Our parents dropped us off at the stage, and we went about our day. These kids are way different than we ever were."

Those problems started at the top. On *Shake It Up* with Chris and Rob, the cast knew who was in charge. Michael, who desperately wanted to be everyone's friend, let the kids run rampant. I became the sheriff, which is never much fun. I will say, however, both casts were hard-working professionals and worked equally hard in the classroom.

Because *Boy Meets World* was such an iconic hit, *Girl Meets World* had massive pre-show press. When an entire cast reads a script for the writers before the actual table read, it's called a pre-table read. Michael felt ours was not very good, from an acting standpoint, so he ripped the younger cast members a new asshole. Michael never said anything bad about Ben for the entire three years and would never say anything bad about Danielle Fishel, our other legacy star, either, at least to her face.

He said the kids were unfocused, marginally talented, and had better pay attention to everything he said, or the show would fail miserably. All that good press they had received to this point was a direct result of *Boy Meets World's* success. They hadn't earned a thing. His insecurities were playing out in plain sight of everyone. Rowan burst into an uncontrollable sobbing fit, which is the way it would go for three more seasons. It would be one crisis after another.

Michael fought with everyone. First and foremost on his list was the Disney creative executive whom he commonly referred to as "Fucky McFuckface." Along the way, he also fought with me, the "Three Wise Men," the writing staff, Danielle, art directors, set decorators, and especially Rowan. Yet still the cast seemingly loved Michael. Nelson, Menell, and Blutman just chalked it up to Stockholm Syndrome, a condition that causes hostages to develop a psychological alliance with their captors as a survival strategy. I steadfastly refused to drink Michael's Kool-Aid.

Writing was a chore as well. On most shows, writers go home on weekends. Not ours. Because Michael was so religious, he would leave on Friday at sundown to observe the Shabbat. We were a Wednesday through Tuesday show, meaning Friday nights were reserved for rewrites based on network notes. We would then shoot on Mondays and Tuesdays. In order to do the rewrite and have Michael observe the Shabbat, the writers also had to retire at sundown Friday and then work Sundays during football season to be ready for Monday morning. Between Michael's stories and the Sunday football games on TV, the writers often took a full day to do what could have been done in four hours or less.

Michael played Rowan's father, Mark Blanchard, like a Stradivarius. Jacobs would grind, grind, grind Mark to get what he wanted out of Rowan. I give Rowan credit. She made it through those tumultuous years with Michael without suffering any psychological damage.

I give her parents credit too. Before anyone reading this says I am being disingenuous, I will be the first to admit that I didn't have a great relationship with Mark Blanchard, especially in the show's first season-and-a-half, which probably affected my relationship with a distant Rowan.

I insisted all parents sit in the bleachers during rehearsals and shows. Mark wanted to be on the floor during rehearsals and behind the cameras on show night. He wanted to spout his wisdom to Rowan or anyone else who would listen. That was never gonna happen on any show that I produced.

Mark was relentless in his efforts and I equally diligent in mine. I am sure my being a prick to Mark must have been quite the topic at the Blanchard family dinner table. Gradually my relationship with Mark became cordial, you could say even friendly.

Things started to settle down when we brought Joel Zwick out of retirement again to direct most of our episodes. Michael and the "Three Wise Men" hated Joel at first because of his Borscht Belt humor and because he picked on Ben. They quickly discovered that he was a terrific director. Plus, he could handle anything that Michael dished out.

Sabrina was a delight, always effervescent and ready to try anything. She and Rowan eventually sang the theme song to our show. Sabrina has gone on to become a great vocal talent and a fine dramatic actress in her own right. Witness her 15,000,000 followers on Instagram. She has two films slated to debut on Netflix in 2020 and 2021.

On the surface, the show was tremendous in every way. There were three Emmy nominations for Best Children's Program in 2014, 15, and 16, plus a Humanitas Prize nomination—the holy grail of writing awards. Producers Guild of America and Writers Guild of America award nominations for Outstanding Children's Programming soon followed.

We had it all, so why did we go off the air?

It is my opinion the same reason we went off the air was the same reason we were on the air. It can be summed up in two words—Michael Jacobs. Disney just got tired of dealing with his crap.

On the bright side, we did find two young, talented directors within the cast. Danielle Fishel directed several episodes flawlessly. From her years on screen, as Topanga, Danielle knew where the jokes were and directed for the camera, a rare combination of skills. Most directors excel at either performance or at blocking cameras, seldom both. Danielle proved the exception. Rider Strong who played Shawn Hunter in both *Boy Meets World* and *Girl Meets World* teamed with his brother Shiloh and proved to be highly capable directors as well. The Strong's along with Danielle take their work seriously and do their homework. I am proud to have played a small part in nurturing their talents. They will deliver quality programming for a long time to come.

The Disney Channel was a great place to work. We had to do more with less, and I loved the challenge. We had almost half the money the major network shows had. The actors were paid less, and we had half the writing staff; but I dare anyone to see the creative difference on the screen.

It was all a good reminder of what one of the Warner Bros. studio execs, Dominick Bruno, had told me years before. They don't pay you for how many hours you work. They pay you for how much you know. As much of a veteran producer as I am, I could not have done the Disney job nearly as well years earlier. I simply wouldn't have had enough experience. I know I never could have pulled off *Murphy Brown* in New York if I hadn't had those Disney years.

"Dream," "try," and "do good" was written on the set of *Girl Meets World*. Those same four magical words summed up my Disney years.

"Dream."

"Try."

"Do Good."

Bella Thorne (l) and Zendaya flank Frank on the set of Shake It Up. I love these girls. (Mitchell Haddad Photography)

A doting Kobe Bryant watches as wife Vanessa and daughters, Gianna and Natalia, bask in Zendaya's and Bella's affection. (Courtesy of Steve Sandoval)

Michael Jacobs and the cast of Girl Meets World. We were nominated for three Emmys from 2014-16. (PF Collection)

"EVERYONE WANTS TO RIDE WITH YOU IN THE LIMO, BUT WHAT YOU WANT IS SOMEONE WHO WILL TAKE THE BUS WITH YOU WHEN THE LIMO BREAKS DOWN."

– Oprah Winfrey

Chapter 15

THE TIES THAT BIND

Here are quick vignettes that add up to a chapter!

Jen & Brad

An odd set of circumstances dropped a Paramount pilot in my lap in the spring of '89. John Masius, an old friend whom I had known since 1973, had written *Ferris Bueller* based on John Hughes's hit film *Ferris Bueller's Day Off*. A postgrad student at UCLA, John and one of my roommates, Don Nesbit, were best friends in "73. I was a department store trainee (don't even ask). We lost touch after John graduated.

Six years later John and I hooked up again when he was one of the producers of *The White Shadow* and I was hawking PONY basketball shoes. John in turn would parlay his success on *The White Shadow* into an executive producer role on *St. Elsewhere*. But I digress. It's 1989, and I don't have an agent. Some guy calls me in the office and says he is an agent.

"Can I represent you for pilot season?" he asks?

"Sure," I replied. "Pilot season only."

"What do I have to lose?"

The agent made one phone call and got John on the phone. Another seven years had passed since I had last spoken to John, but as soon as the agent said my name, John hired me on the spot. The shocked agent couldn't wait to tell me that I got the job on his first phone call. We produced a fine pilot with a delightful cast and sold the pilot to NBC.

Masius, the cast, and I all got along great, but I was contractually bound to go back to *Head of The Class*. John offered me a piece of the back end to stay, but *Head of the Class* had taken a gamble on me.

I felt obliged to turn down John's offer.

Good thing for loyalty.

We shot two more seasons of *HOTC*, while Ferris was canceled after thirteen episodes. John later created and produced long-running hits *Touched by an Angel* and *Providence.*

The young actress who played Ferris Bueller's sister Jeannie also thrived. Years later, I spotted her on the Warner Bros lot. Breaking away from her castmates on *Friends,* Jennifer Aniston hugged me like a long-lost brother.

One thing I will say about my pal, John Masius, he could spot talent.

In *Head of the Class's* third season, after we returned from Moscow, there was still almost an entire season to shoot. For the tenth episode that season, we shot "The Problem with Maria" and cast a young guest star who had recently arrived in L.A. from Missouri to guest star opposite series regular Leslie Bega. Usually guest stars get paid scale, which was then maybe $2,300 per week. They come in for the table read on Monday, rehearse all week, shoot the show on Friday, and no one ever hears from them again. (Remember what I said about an actor's life?) No one really has time to get close. This kid was different. Women came to the stage in droves and went absolutely gaga for this unknown. I didn't get it. He was nice-looking, sure, but I didn't see the intangibles. I guess maybe I didn't see the tangibles either.

That episode, the kid played the athlete Chuck. Maria feared her superior IQ would intimidate him. The usual episodic tomfoolery occurred, and we got the show in the can. The episode was just okay. That ordinary episode turned extraordinary years later when the actor who played Chuck—Brad Pitt—became famous. Brad became one of the biggest stars in show business; his celebrity grew even more exponentially when he married, of all people, the aforementioned Jennifer Aniston.

JB: The Goat

Who is the Greatest of All Time?

In basketball you can argue that is Michael, LeBron, Kareem, or any number of names. In golf, you can argue Tiger, Jack, or Arnie. When it comes to the GOAT of catchers, everyone's pick is Johnny Lee Bench from Binger, Oklahoma. Johnny was a fourteen-time All-star with the Cincinnati Reds, played on two world championship teams, and was twice named the National League's MVP.

I first met Johnny in 1999 in Lexington, Kentucky. He was co-hosting a children's charity celebrity golf tournament with former Reds and Mets second baseman Doug "The Glue" Flynn. For some unknown reason, I was asked to appear as a celebrity. Johnny and I hit it off right away. I guess the fact that I represented Rod Carew probably didn't hurt my cause. Those two superstars really respected one another.

Over the years, Karen and I returned to Kentucky annually. Johnny and I also ran into each other at Hall of Fame inductions or at various card shows around the country. After the card shows, Rod usually retired early, so Bench and I would often have dinner. Our bond grew stronger as Johnny would reminisce about his two young sons, Justin and Josh. At the age when other people were becoming grandfathers, Johnny delighted in doting on his two boys, whether it was doing their laundry, taking them to school, or coaching little league baseball. "JB" is still always there.

An after-dinner speaker, country singer, comedian, and carnival barker for multiple products, Johnny Bench is more than a baseball legend. He's one hell of a storyteller. Let me share one of my favorites.

Johnny's dad was a pretty good baseball player. On Saturdays, a young Johnny would religiously watch baseball's *Game of the Week* while his dad would stroll by the TV, glance at the game, point his chin upwards toward the pitcher, and boast, "Ah can hit that guy."

Johnny believed him. Lo and behold, before his teenage years ended, Johnny was in the Majors. His rookie year he faced Bob Gibson, an assassin on the mound and one of the greatest pitchers of any generation. Gibson zipped the first fastball right past Johnny for a strike. Then Gibson threw a second followed by the third strike. Bench froze, never taking the bat off his shoulder. While Bench laughed on his long stroll back to the dugout, his manager Dave Bristol fumed, "What the hell is so funny?"

Johnny smirked. "No way Dad hits that guy."

In January 2013, as noted previously, I suffered a stroke, a dissected carotid. The odds of my survival were maybe one in five. By the hand of God, I made it. During my three months of recuperation, Johnny Bench called almost every week. I could barely speak. I would try to say something, get frustrated, and finally just say, "Ah shit." Johnny would just laugh. Week after week, he would call. As my condition improved our conversations got longer and longer. For being there when I needed him most, and even more importantly, for his profound sense of humanity, to me Johnny Bench will always be so, so much more than the greatest catcher of all time.

The Doc and Kid Johnny

Quick, name a person with a PhD in neuroscience.

It may be easier to pick a star of your favorite television show, but can you pick a person who is both? I can. Dr. Mayim Bialik, co-star of *The Big Bang Theory*.

I first met Mayim when she was cast as the fourteen-year-old star of a pilot I was producing for Fox called *Molloy*. I really hadn't heard about her, but when my executive producer Grant Rosenberg told me she had played the young Bette Midler in *Beaches*, I knew exactly who she was. She was *goood*.

A pilot schedule is similar to a series schedule except the cast and the director have seven days to rehearse and shoot, rather than the usual five. Mayim didn't need the extra days. She was "off book" (knew her lines) from day one, which is extraordinary considering she would have to relearn newly rewritten lines every day. No problem for Mayim. Every night we would deliver the script, and by morning, she was "off book." We were clueless to how smart she was. Her mom Beverly and father Barry were extremely supportive and there with her every step. Mayim was perfect in every way.

We shot the pilot, and it sold. It would air on the Fox network. The pilot completed, again, I headed back to *Head of the Class*. Comedy is difficult and not always so rewarding. After only six episodes, *Molloy* was canceled. The rewards came later for Mayim. Free from her *Molloy* obligations, Mayim quickly got another show called *Blossom,* which ran for five full seasons, or 114 episodes. Mayim wanted more out of life, so she left show business. I didn't really hear about her for five or six years. Mayim had enrolled at UCLA and completed in record time her undergraduate, master's, and PhD requirements. I figured I had heard the last of her.

Johnny Galecki, meanwhile, knew he wanted to be an actor from the early age of three. By the time he did the pilot for *Billy*, a *Head of the Class* spin-off starring Scottish stand-up comic Billy Connolly,

Johnny's career was already taking off. Billy Connolly had replaced Howard Hesseman as the teacher in *HOTC*. He performed so spectacularly that instead of bringing back the show for a sixth season, with some of the actors approaching thirty, ABC canceled the show and picked up a series written specifically for him. In the show, Billy would move from New York to Berkeley and live in the basement of a home with a widowed mom and her two children. The concept for the show was loosely based on the movie *Green Card*.

Johnny was a delight, as was Billy and the rest of the cast. But comedy is hard. Where have I heard that before? *Billy* got its walking papers from the network after thirteen episodes. Johnny was undaunted.

Despite being only 5'5", Johnny Galecki was in demand. He worked constantly in movie and TV roles. He was *goood* too. One thing led to another, and in 2007, Johnny was cast in his career-defining role as Leonard Hofstadter in the seminal hit *The Big Bang Theory*.

By 2010, Mayim, now in her mid-thirties, had two children and her PhD and was working long hours away from her kids. How can I spend more time with them and still make a living, she wondered? The answer was easy. She would return to acting. Some people would have been intimidated at the thought. Not Mayim.

She was cast as a guest star in *The Big Bang Theory* as Dr. Amy Farrah Fowler, Sheldon (Jim Parson's) love interest. That guest shot landed her a spot as a series regular by season four. Mayim Bialik's life was set.

In season eight, the five original stars held out in tandem for a reported $1 million an episode, which would turn into $24 million for *each* of them for the season. Warner's met their demands—what could they do? The show was the number one show on television. Two seasons later, the five took a $100,000 per episode pay cut each to upgrade both Mayim and Melissa Rauch's salaries. That unselfishness is unheard of in our business. Mayim and Rauch had joined the cast earning $175,000 per episode. They were bumped to a reported $425,000 per episode. Not bad work if you can get it.

Johnny Galecki and Mayim Bialik had found that pot of gold over the same rainbow. Good for them. Sometimes good things do happen to *goood* people.

Rita and Cowboy Joe

Racquetball? You might remember racquetball. It was the fastest-growing sport in the late '70s and early '80s. Now, not so much.

I was going around the country promoting a pro racquetball tour for our client Ektelon in 1978 when I met a player on the circuit named Rita Hoff.

Rita had been a great basketball player in college and later would be voted into the Missouri Sports Hall of Fame for her accomplishments. A terrific all-around athlete, Rita was a pretty fine racquetball player who was trying to excel in a new sport. At the time, women's racquetball was dominated by two players, Shannon Wright and Jennifer Harding. Rita never could beat those two in the same tournament, but she was good enough at one time to rank in the top six nationally and be voted into the Racquetball Hall of Fame in 2006.

As time marched , another player Jean Sauser, Rita and I remained friends. To this day Rita and I call each other "Cheezburga, Cheezburga," referencing the famous John Belushi line from *Saturday Night Live*. Sauser and I are both firmly rooted in *Beverly Hillbillies* trivia.

Several years ago, Rita met Cowboy Joe West, the dean of Major League umpires, a lively, enigmatic character, to say the least. Check the player's poll of the best and worst umpires in the league, and Joe tops *both* lists. Lots of players love Joe. Others, well, again I say, look at the poll. Joe is polarizing. People often call me an acquired taste, so is Joe. Rita acquired that taste and married Joe in 2018.

Karen and I started spending time with Rita and Joe in Pebble Beach in 2015. After each major league season, they would come to the famed resort to play in baseball's World Series of Golf. Rita also traveled with Joe, so we would see them on trips to L.A. and then to New York when I was there for *Murphy Brown*.

As an umpire, Joe obviously knew Johnny Bench and Rod Carew, so we became fast friends. Like Johnny, Joe is a raconteur and got his nickname "Cowboy Joe" because he is a fine country singer. He even hosts his own country music show on Sirius Radio. Hell, Joe even performed at the Grand Ole Opry, the holy grail for country singers.

Once he puts the uniform on, all singing and fun stops. Joe is all business and arguably the game's finest caller of balls and strikes. As of this writing, Joe has umpired 5,310 major league games. The record of 5,369 is held by the legendary Hall of Fame umpire Bill Klem, who retired in 1951. Joe is now sixty-seven years old and nearing retirement. He was hoping to break the record for most games umpired sometime in July 2020. Now, with the COVID-19 pandemic raging, the question is will he break the record at all? He needs fifty-nine games but has only been cleared physically for one more year. The 2021 season for Joe is in doubt.

Joe has never been the darling of the MLB administration. When the umpires went out on strike in 1999, Joe led the surge. Joe became president of the umpires' union in 2009 and negotiated the largest contract for umpires in baseball history. The umpires gained many benefits that the league never would have granted without Joe's leadership. I don't think it would break the hearts of MLB officials if Joe fell short of Bill Klem's record. They might even some day lobby against Joe's well-earned induction into the Hall of Fame.

Hopefully by the time this book is published, the baseball season will have started, and Joe will be on his way to breaking the record. I had hoped to fly in for the game. That will never happen now. The record will most probably be broken in a stadium with no fans. Although a pyrrhic victory for Joe, I am sure he would have liked to acknowledge the cheers (and a few boos) of the fans, it will be a victory, nonetheless.

One thing I am sure of: If all pandemic restrictions are lifted, and God willing we all live, come the week after Thanksgiving, the raucous foursome in the corner booth having cocktails in Pebble Beach and having beaucoup fun will be the Pace's and the West's.

It's Me, It's Me, It's Ernest T.

One of my many mentors on the way up was Howie Morris. You probably know him best as Ernest T. Bass on *The Andy Griffith Show*. Older readers would remember Howie as one of TV's pioneers on *Your Show of Shows*, which starred Sid Caesar, Carl Reiner, Imogene Coca, and Howie. The show's writing staff included Woody Allen, Neil Simon, Selma Diamond, and Larry Gelbart—not too shabby. No one who saw it could forget Howie's famous skit with Sid as Uncle Goopy. Google that classic, "This Is Your Life."

Howard was maybe 5'6" on a good day, but no one gave him shit.

He had a mouth on him that could make a sailor blush.

It got so during our years together I thought my name was "Guinea Prick."

The streets of New York had made him fearless.

That is what I liked about him.

I learned how to work from Howard as I also learned how *not* to work.

Howie's father had lost his job during the Depression. He died a short term later of what Howie said was "unemployment."

Howie broke into radio by impersonating inanimate objects, such as boxing gloves and chopping blocks. (Think about that for a second). He made his Broadway debut in the role of Puck in *A Midsummer's Night Dream* and went on to become a noted director of feature films, commercials, and television. He was also the voice of hundreds of cartoon characters, including the Quantas airline's koala bear.

Howie directed the pilot of *Get Smart*, which was created by another *Your Show of Shows* writer, Mel Brooks. The first time Howard met Mel Brooks, Sid had introduced Brooks as a writer from France. Monsieur Brie was here to study American writers and spoke no English. Howie said they would just nod hello and say "bonjour" upon passing in the hallway. About a week in, Howie was taking a piss when Monsieur Brie stepped into the urinal next to him. Howie nodded his usual hello, but instead of his usual greeting, Monsieur Brie countered with, "How they hangin', Howie?"

When they both cracked up, a lifetime friendship was born.

Howie and I had a short-lived but successful commercial production company in the mid '80s, founded in partnership with director Howard Storm. On one particular shoot for Chevy, we had 250 extras, dressed as clowns, ball players, marching band members, jugglers, and court jesters, and two cars on a loading dock in Long Beach. We were supposed to believe they were all coming out of one pallet box. It would take all of Howie's directorial talents. I was nervous. As Howie mounted his camera crane, he looked over to me with mischief in his eye and asked, "Now what do we do?" We delivered a damned fine commercial, that's what we did. After we all got busy on other projects, Howie and I remained good friends. We'd have lunch together often, sometimes two or three times a month. We even used Howie as a special guest star in several sitcoms. He was the mensch of mensches.

Divorced five times, Howard Morris fell in and out of love repeatedly and once asked me how many times can a man subdivide? After his third marriage failed, Howard said he was remarrying his second wife, Dolores, and laughingly said he should announce the wedding in *The Recycler*.

The thing I miss most about Howard is that he could find humor in anything. After his father's death, Howard went down the Hudson

River to scatter his father's ashes. A strong breeze blew his dad's ashes onto Howard's good suit. When Mel Brooks asked Howard, "Where do you consider your father's final resting place to be?", Howard shot back, "I would have to say Grand Cleaners on Park Avenue."

Do not go gentle into that good night, my friend. I know you didn't.

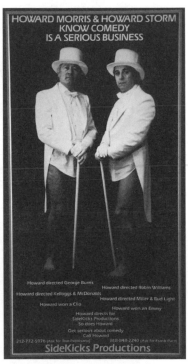

"It's me, it's me, it's Earnest T" played brilliantly on the Andy Griffith Show by Howie Morris. (Courtesy of Howard Morris)

An ad for the commercial production company, Howie, Director Howard Storm, and I had in the early 1980s. (PF Collection)

The GOAT of catchers, Johnny Bench (center). Behind him are former MLB standout Doug "The Glue" Flynn, UK Head Women's Basketball Coach Matthew Mitchell, Artis Gilmore, myself, and Artis' Jacksonville University teammate, Bob Nylin. (Courtesy of Children's Charity of the Bluegrass)

Mayim was fourteen when she did Malloy...pictured here with Executive Producer Grant Rosenberg, Bari Halle, and myself. (PF Collection)

A young Jennifer Aniston (lower right) starred in Fox TV's series Ferris Bueller. You may have heard of her. (Courtesy, Getty Images)

"WISE MEN TALK BECAUSE THEY HAVE SOMETHING TO SAY. FOOLS TALK BECAUSE THEY HAVE TO SAY SOMETHING."

– Plato

Chapter 16

JOHN WAYNE – AN AUTHENTIC AMERICAN HERO

If America had a Mount Rushmore of popular culture, John Wayne would be front and center. He was always larger-than-life. Even now, more than forty years after his death, his star still shines as bright as when Wayne was America's top box office draw.

Don't believe me? Google "who are America's most popular movie stars?".

Even though his last movie *The Shootist*, was released nearly a half a century ago, John Wayne still comes in fourth. That's right. Directly behind Denzel Washington, just ahead of Harrison Ford, and an astonishing six spots ahead of Brad Pitt.

"The Duke" has held a spot in that top-ten list for this entire century.

In this bewildering age of texting and Twitter, celebrities have a penchant for shortening their names: Madonna, Beyoncé, J. Lo, Jay Z, and on and on. If Wayne were alive today, he'd be 113 years old and in his own words, "Nobody ever really calls me John. I've always been Duke or Marion or John Wayne. It's a name that goes well together, and it's like one word—JohnWayne."

In 1978, much like the Duke, sports played a huge role in society. Bucky Dent broke the Red Sox hearts; Reggie Jackson soon did the same to the Dodgers; Affirmed and Alydar waged three races for the ages from Churchill Downs to Pimlico to Belmont. Ali regained the heavyweight title, Gary Player won the Masters, Rod Carew captured his seventh batting title, and, oh, Kobe Bryant was born.

So great was John Wayne's influence that, in the '70s, the NFL official football was called "The Duke." It still is today, I might add.

Somehow the inaugural Ektelon-Natural Light Racquetball Championships got lost in all that sporting news. This is where John

Wayne enters this picture. Hold on. Bear with me a second. I know what you're thinking.

What the hell is he talking about? This guy Pace is as crazy as a sprayed roach. What in the hell does a long-forgotten racquetball tournament have to do with John Wayne?

Trust me, plenty.

I met Wayne in 1978, a couple years out of my two-year stint as a PR guy in the defunct World Football League. Surely you remember the Southern California Sun, the Portland Storm, and the Chicago Winds? No? Well, I do. I worked for all of them.

After the WFL, I accepted a job as PR director for The Phillips Organisation Ltd., a San Diego-based marketing firm specializing in clients within the sporting goods industry. TPO's biggest client was Ektelon, a manufacturer on the cutting edge of racquetball, a sport that was a phenomenon for about ten years, starting in the mid-70s, until its popularity eventually waned.

Racquetball was chic and fun. Everybody wanted in, including Anheuser Busch; thus, the Ektelon-Natural Light Championships were born.

I conceived the event, supported by a young writer named Armen Keteyian who had been posting high school sports scores on page nine of an eight-page sports section of the *Escondido Times-Advocate* newspaper when we hired him.

One of our main responsibilities was to work with the brewery, which had bought its way into racquetball prominence by virtue of a check for $250,000. A key element to the tournament's format was an agreement between Ektelon and Busch that a portion of any proceeds from the national tournament would be donated to the American Heart Association. One of their spokespeople was John Wayne.

The American Heart Association had always made it clear to us that Wayne would have no involvement in the event, none whatsoever. Somehow, when check presentation time arrived, schedules shifted, and the stars aligned to allow Wayne to accept the check at his home. We were told that all we had to do was show up. The folks from Anheuser Busch would handle everything.

I remember calling my dad, a World War II veteran, and telling him that I was going to John Wayne's house. Wayne was my dad's favorite actor. My dad couldn't have been more excited had he been meeting Wayne himself.

When the day arrived, Ektelon vice president Ron Grimes and I met in San Diego for the seventy-five-minute drive north to Newport Beach.

As we approached Wayne's house, I was surprised at how accessible it was. There was no guard gate, no security. Just a house at the end of Bayshore Drive as the directions suggested. Wayne lived in a large white ranch-style home overlooking Newport Bay. Ironically, the ten-bedroom house stood only a mile or so from the Balboa Pier, where a body surfing injury some fifty years earlier had cost Marion Morrison his football scholarship at USC, forcing him into a $35-a-week job as a prop hand at 20th Century Fox.

While Morrison was moving furniture at Fox, storied film director John Ford spotted him, and the legend of John Wayne was born. One hundred and forty movies would follow in a career that spanned forty-six years and included three Academy Award nominations and an Oscar win for *True Grit* in 1970.

Once at the house, a lovely woman by the name of Pat Stacy welcomed us. Stacy, who appeared to be in her mid-forties, introduced herself as Mr. Wayne's assistant.

Stacy escorted us into the backyard and asked us to wait while she went inside to tell Wayne we had arrived. Her one request was that we don't ask for autographs. The backyard was beautifully manicured, framed by the blue water of the bay and centered by a spectacular pool. Beyond the pool was a dock where Wayne's yacht, *The Wild Goose*, a 135-foot converted mine-sweeper, was moored.

We walked up the steps leading to the pool and turned toward the house, where the curtains behind French doors were closed. After a short wait, the curtains drew open, as did the sliding glass door.

And there he stood, filling the doorway.

The man Ronald Reagan said "gave the whole world the image of what an American should be."

The man Pulitzer Prize-winning author and historian Gary Willis called "the most popular movie star ever."

The man *New York Times* film critic Vincent Canby decreed was "marvelously indestructible."

The man my father idolized.

There in the doorway stood "The Duke" himself.

Wayne's participation stemmed from his sense of duty having survived heart surgery years earlier. There were probably many other places he would rather have been that Sunday afternoon. Yet he was amiable enough as he strode out and did the perfunctory greetings.

Here I stood with John Wayne and Grimes. When Grimes mistakenly placed his hand on Wayne's shoulder, The Duke snarled, "What are ya trying to do, make love to me?"

I remember thinking that his sports coat was a bit big, not realizing that the cancer, which would claim his life a year later at age seventy-two, had already begun to ravish his body. (Note to reader: To best enjoy what follows, read the hero's quotes in your best John Wayne voice and picture the majesty of his swagger in every step).

Pointing to a spot by the pool, Wayne motioned, "Let's take the photo over there."

Then it happened.

It was the moment the sun stopped shining.

It was the moment the earth stopped rotating.

It was the moment that all life as we knew it ceased to exist.

The *it* was the arrogant voice that interrupted. "No. I think it would look better over here."

The words had come from my PR counterpart from Anheuser Busch, a young woman in her mid-twenties, the same person who was going to "take care of everything."

I watched the color drain from Pat Stacy's face as I braced myself, hoping we would survive the next ten seconds. We wouldn't. After what seemed like an eternity, Wayne erupted. "Fifty years in the damn picture business, fifty years! You think by now I'd know how to take a g*d damned snapshot. Take the f**king picture anywhere you want Miss Artiste, but you're taking it without me."

With that he turned and did the inimitable John Wayne tilted strut back toward the house. The sliding glass doors closed. The curtains shut, and just like that, he and Pat disappeared.

The gal from the beer company was clearly neutered. Her work was done for the day. As we stood in stunned silence, the photographer started gathering his gear. "Hold on," I said. I looked at Grimes. He looked back and raised his head toward the house, as if to say, "Go ahead. Take your best shot."

I timidly knocked on the slider, hoping Pat's head would appear rather than you-know whose. Thankfully, I got my wish. The curtain pulled back slightly, the door opened about two feet, and I asked Pat, "What do we do now? Any chance of saving this?"

She invited me in. This time the curtains and the door closed behind me.

"Wait here," she said in a comforting tone. "Let me see what I can do."

I was in John Wayne's den. Just me, all by myself. The room was darkened to protect its contents from the damaging rays of the setting afternoon sun. The den was paneled in a rich, dark wood. An oil painting of Wayne was over the fireplace. There was the Duke in his prime, dressed in his cowboy finest—ten-gallon hat atop his head, bandana around his neck, strapping and self-assured.

I had never before seen a portrait so lifelike, so perfectly painted, so perfectly lit. Original Remington sculptures of the Old West further decorated the room. If it seemed like a museum, well, maybe that's because in a way it was.

I hadn't yet taken in all the treasures of the room when Pat returned. "He'll do it," she said. "But no one is to speak to him. You'll take the picture and leave as quickly as possible. Now if you can wait by the pool, he'll be out in a moment." She couldn't have been any sweeter.

I thanked her and hurried to ready the group. I assembled everyone by the pool, where Wayne had suggested we take the photo in the first place. The curtain opened one last time. Wayne approached for take two. To say the air was thick with tension would be an understatement. True to my agreement with Pat Stacy, not a word was spoken.

After the photo was shot, Wayne looked at the racquet in his hand and said, "What the hell is this?"

"It's a gift for your grandchildren," I volunteered quickly.

Just then, a representative from the American Heart Association arrived poolside.

"Who the hell are you?" Wayne asked.

"I'm from the American Heart Association," she said.

Wayne looked at the woman who had obviously come directly from the hairdresser and said, "Well, here's your damn check, and take this, too," handing her the racquet. With that he turned and sashayed off into the sunset.

Wayne once famously said, "Nobody should come to the movies unless he believes in heroes." When you paid to see the Duke, that's what you paid for and that's what you got, the big tough guy on the side of right, the man who epitomized the phrase "a man's gotta do what a man's gotta do."

That night, as soon as I put my key into the lock to open my front door, the phone started ringing. It was Dad.

"Did you go John Wayne's house?"

"Sure did," I replied.

"How was he?"

I took a short beat and remembered that "a man's gotta do what a man's gotta do," so I gave Dad the only answer I could.

"Pop," I said, "he was the best."

"I knew he would be," Dad said. "He's John Wayne."

No so fast, pilgrim. John Wayne and the infamous photo with Ektelon VP Ron Grimes. (Courtesy of Ron Grimes)

Armen Keteyian (r) was the voice of racquetball in the early 1980s. He became a best selling author and multi-Emmy Award winning journalist. (PF Collection)

"SUCCESS IS ACHIEVED BY THOSE OF US NOT OBSESSED WITH SELF-AWARENESS."

— Author unknown

Chapter 17

THE CRAFTSMEN

I Love Lucy set the standard for the modern sitcom and refined the multiple-camera format, which had its genesis only years before on *Amos and Andy*. Director Desi Arnaz was a visionary. He was the first to shoot a show with a studio audience. He was the first to record the audience's natural laughs. Desi set in motion innovative new ways of dressing sets, lighting the actors, and laying down the audio. Desi's way was a much quicker and less expensive way to shoot shows.

In Desi's world, the couch always faces the audience. In my world too. Otherwise you can't see the actor's full faces. In future years, on rehearsal days, many first-time sitcom directors would try to change the location of the couch. I would just sit back and knowingly smile. When the cameramen came in, they would see what I had seen. They knew they couldn't shoot the scene as conceived. The director wasn't directing for the cameras. He always had to come back to Desi's way.

The front door was never in the back of an Arnaz set. It was always on the left or the right. Otherwise, you can't see the person's face answering the door. It's the same way in my world, entrance stage left or stage right.

The craftsmen who work behind the scenes are some of the most critical in the business. They can't afford one slipup. If they do, you will notice. If an actor is holding a drink in his left hand in one take and in his right the next, you will notice. Blame the script supervisor. If a microphone dips into a shot, you'll see it. That's on the sound person. If an actress comes back after lunch with a slightly different hairstyle, blame the stylist.

Now, admit it.

You really don't pay much attention to the credits at the end of a movie or a television show. Unless you live in Los Angeles, the feature credits are to your back as you exit the movie theater. As soon as the TV credits start to roll, you're either on your way to the refrigerator, to the bathroom, or to the remote.

Every credit has a person behind it, and every person has a story. The folks in the end credits are the heart and soul of the film business. Without them, Jennifer Lawrence, Bradley Cooper, or The Rock could just as easily be your co-worker.

Before we talk about who the craftsmen are, let's talk a little more about what some of them do.

Many of their job titles go back hundreds of years to the English theater. The rear of the set is called "upstage" because the sets were slightly elevated so that audience members could see the actors better. Moving upstage or downstage became common terminology, first in theater and later in films and television.

The titles that seem to reap the most curiosity are the grips, gaffers, and the boom men. As had been tradition since ancient Greece, English theaters used sailors in the seventeenth and eighteenth centuries as the main workforce to prepare their stages. Most of today's more unique job designations evolved from terms used by those sailors to describe either the parts of a ship or the tools they used at sea.

When lights became necessary in theaters, men set them up and moved them with big iron hooks secured to long shafts. These "gaff poles" were originally designed for landing large fish. Because a gaffer is another term for grandfather, or godfather, the combination of the two led the chief stage electrician to be called "the gaffer."

Working alongside the gaffer were handymen who helped to secure the lights and sets. As these sailors evolved into stagehands, they became known as "grips," referring to the bag sailors used to carry tools around ships.

The extended pole supporting the microphone over an actor's head, occasionally dipping into the shot, is called the boom. This term derived from the boom of a ship or the horizontal pole used to extend the foot of a sail or to handle cargo. The holder of the boom is predictably called the boom man.

A Hollywood craftsman's life involves a regimen of hourly, daily, and weekly mundane jobs, but even if successful, they have minimum security. Even the elite ones have to cope with virtually no income during the three-month production hiatus factored into every television season. There are work stoppages, union labor strikes, and now even the COVID-19 pandemic. You certainly can not work from home if you are a craftsman. Lots of folks I know lost their careers during the 100-day work stoppage in 2008. Lots more will lose their jobs in 2020. Susette Hsuing, executive vice president of network production for Disney, told me she had to lay off thousands of below-the-line craftsmen during the COVID-19 pandemic. Heartbreaking.

Let's roll a few credits and meet some pretty fascinating people:

Name: Kate Wright
Job: Script Supervisor
Union Salary: $2,100 per week (when working)*

Kate Wright never expected to become a script supervisor, yet here she is monitoring the accuracy of cast dialogue and keeping up with the many scripts changes furiously being rewritten between takes. She also is charged with making sure everything is the same from take to take. It's a big job.

Born in Toronto, Kate began dancing professionally at fifteen. Within a week of her high school graduation, she headed to New York, where for the next twelve years Kate succeeded in establishing herself as one of the most dependable dancers in Broadway musical theater, highlighted by her three-year run as Sheila in *A Chorus Line*.

Dancers, like professional athletes, have a short shelf life but without the enormous paydays. After ten years of eight shows a week, Kate knew it was time for a change.

"I was thirty and wanted to get married and have babies." Wright's mouth curved into a smile. "Two things that don't fit into the grueling demands of a dancer's life, plus it beats you up physically. I moved to California and was able to pick up periodic work as a choreographer on shows like *Roseanne*. After my kids were born, I knew I needed something steadier."

A chance meeting with a script supervisor on *The Player* led Wright to a class in that discipline, which in turn led to volunteer work on student films and finally her smooth segue into situation comedies. She has become one of the best in the business.

"It was hard to give up dancing," she said, her forehead creasing. "It was part of my soul. Being behind the camera is different than being in front of it, but I'm still in the business, and I couldn't be happier."

(*All salaries based on 2020 union rate cards)

Name: Steve Wollenberg
Job: Camera Utility—Video Tape
Union Salary: $44.44 per eight-hour day (when working)
First Job: *Centennial,* assistant cameraman

You learned a little about Steve in Billy's introduction. I never start any show without hiring Wollenberg. A loyal and tireless worker who at even now in his 70's can outpace any two men. I would wager he can kick their asses as well. A quick story.

When Mike Tyson was still the undefeated heavyweight champion of the world, back in the late '80s, Mike was on the *Head of the Class* stage to see Robin. I asked Steve if he thought he could take him in a fight.

"I don't know who would win a fight between us." Steve, the former Vietnam vet, grinned. "But I am sure of one thing. Put us both twenty miles behind enemy lines. Within an hour, I'd be out of the jungle, and Mike would be hanging upside down from a tree."

One of the most literate people I have ever met, Wollenberg reads James Joyce's epic novel *Ulysses* every two years just to make sure he hasn't forgotten anything. Steve is a jack-of-all trades who belongs to five unions and is more than qualified to go above and beyond. In addition, Steve has acted on several television series, including *George Lopez* and *ER.* A true renaissance man, Steve is one of a kind.

Name: Mike Kelly
Job: Assistant Director
Union Salary: $5,300 per week (again, when working)
Aspiration: Director

The irrefutable reality of the entertainment industry is that there is no middle class. Some people make obscene amounts of money while the majority live from paycheck to paycheck. As a salaried middle-class employee, the assistant director (AD) is one of the few exceptions.

A top notch AD can make upwards of $150,000 a year. Mike Kelly describes his job as "the eye of the hurricane." One who keeps his head while others are losing theirs. The AD works with the director and the producer to plan the most effective manner, creatively and financially, to shoot a show. He then assimilates that information and communicates it quickly and precisely to all appropriate department heads.

It's not surprising that Mike Kelly ended up in show business. His father, Fred, was one of Broadway's most revered directors, and his uncle, Gene Kelly, had been known to dance around a movie set or two.

"Even though I graduated from Marquette with a degree in philosophy," said Kelly, "I think I always knew I'd end up in show business. Having a famous last name didn't hurt, but ultimately I had to make it on my own. Most people don't understand that anyone can learn what the equipment does and figure out how to fill out the paperwork. It's people skills that determine your success. This is a very political business."

Although he has successfully directed several network television episodes, Kelly sees his window of opportunity as a director closing quickly. Yet he remains optimistic and upbeat.

"This life hasn't been easy, but I have a wonderful wife of forty years and four fantastic kids. Those are five great reasons to keep going, to keep trying, and to do the best I can."

He gave a half smile.

"Yes, there have been dry periods without working, but we don't overextend ourselves. We aren't extravagant people, so we always make it through. People respected my dad and my Uncle Gene. The two of them loved their work, and I'm lucky enough to say I've followed in their footsteps." Mike is currently developing a stage play on his life entitled *Growing Up Kelly*.

Name: Reilly Richardson
Age: 26
Job: Actor Stand-In/Understudy
Salary: $195 per eight-hour day
Aspiration: Broadway actress

Reilly was born in Lexington, Kentucky, and was bitten by the acting bug at an early age. She went to a performing arts high school and graduated from the Musical Theatre program at the University of Michigan. Upon graduation, she immediately moved to New York and soon found out that she wasn't alone.

She has faced the same challenges as the others: no agent, no work, and little money. Many pick up a few days' work as "background atmosphere," a fancy phrase for "extra." Just one of the many mute faces that populate scenes requiring lots of people.

That wasn't for Reilly. She made the right decision.

Once you get typed as an extra, it is hard to break out. She found it necessary to supplement her income by getting a mundane job waiting tables. It was not what she wanted to do, but bills don't pay themselves. She knew that being a waitress would give her more flexible hours for those days when she was called for an audition.

"Auditions are hard," said Reilly over a cup of coffee. "But I've learned that as long as you avoid taking rejection personally, you have a chance to survive until you get your break."

In 2018, Reilly caught her first break. She was hired to be Faith Ford's stand-in on *Murphy Brown*. She finally had a place to go every day to earn a steady paycheck. She was so good that she was even cast for a small role in an episode. For that she received her SAG card. She still, however, doesn't have an agent. Alas, *Murphy Brown* was canceled after one season, yet Reilly used her contacts and the people she met on set wisely. I'll wager that the world will soon hear from Reilly Richardson.

Name: Steve Trainor
Job: Best Boy Electric
Union Salary: $2,879 per week (when working)
First Job: *Batman II*

When Steve Trainor was a boy, he didn't expect to be celebrating his fortieth birthday rigging lights. He expected to retire from a distinguished career as a Major League Baseball player. For a while, he was on his way.

"I'd pitched my way into a Division-I baseball scholarship at San Diego State," said Trainor. "Following my junior year, I'd never had a losing season or an ERA above 3.90. I played in the Jayhawk League between the summer of my junior and senior year and was 7-3 as a starter with a 2.47 ERA. A lot of promises were made but none were kept."

After a disappointing senior year and a couple of seasons kicking around the Independent Minor Leagues, Trainor decided to get on with his life.

"I never had that great a fastball," he recalls. "I had good mechanics and great control, but I could see that there were a lot of guys like me. I wanted to leave before the game left a bad taste in my mouth."

Trainor refocused his efforts and returned to school, where he completed his coursework and graduated from San Diego State.

"When I was a kid, I had a neighbor who worked for the studios. He liked me and told me if baseball didn't work out and I ever wanted to get in at the studios, I should just ask. After graduation, I didn't think I was cut out for any management training jobs, so I called him." Trainor crossed his arms across his chest and his mouth broke into a wide grin.

"About two hours later, he called me back and said if I was really serious, he had a job for me. 'Show up tomorrow at 5 a.m. with a pair of gloves, a wrench, a screwdriver, and a good attitude.' I showed up the next day with my batting gloves because that's all I had, but the guys I worked with liked my attitude, the way I listened, and the way I got along with people. Everything just snowballed from there."

Today as the best boy electric, Trainor works as the gaffer's right-hand man. He's the "best boy" managing the lighting manpower and equipment on the set.

"I guess being a journeyman and playing on so many teams all those years has paid off after all," mused Trainor.

Name: Barry Harvey
Position: Craft Services
Salary: $40.28 per hour, 54 pay hours guaranteed per week
First Job: *Compromising Positions*

Movie companies and armies move on their stomachs. Someone has to feed the cast and crew, and that food better be good. By definition the craft service department, or "crafty" for short, services the crafts. It provides food, drinks, gum, and other snacks, and it's affiliated with the International Alliance of Theatrical Stage Employees.

The craft service people show up on the sound stage by 5 a.m. or earlier to prepare breakfast for up to 120 people. They cook the eggs, fry the bacon, prepare the oatmeal, slice the bagels, and cut up the fruit. They and their assistants often stay until after the show wraps to clean up. On show night, they'll often hang around after the show to organize a bootleg penny-ante card game or to provide a forbidden beer or cocktail.

Barry Harvey never thought he would be a crafty. He was groomed to be a restaurateur back home in Connecticut as the third generation, son of a son of a son. He attended one semester at UConn before he packed up and moved to L.A., where he worked the kitchen at Pizza Hut.

Working hard to fulfill his forefathers' expectations, Barry finally opened his own restaurant. Then he sustained a major head injury in a near fatal car accident, which forced him to abandon his lifelong dream. Fate stepped in again when he met a TV producer at a baseball card collector's show. (It wasn't me). They hit it off, and after learning of Barry's history in the food business, the producer offered him a non-union craft service job on his TV show.

That led to a craft services job as a "day player" on *The Practice*. A day player is someone who gets called to work for one session. That same morning, the craft service man got a call to interview for *The Tracey Ullman Show*. Not wanting to leave his secure job, the craft service guy sent Barry instead. Barry was offered the non-union job, which soon went union.

Barry was in.

Harvey has worked nonstop ever since. He is likable and dependable, and as anyone from the set of *Will & Grace* can tell you, his food is great.

Name: Steve Dorff
Job: Music Composer
First Job: *Any Which Way but Loose*

F, F-sharp. F, F-sharp. Two notes over and over again, relentless, unstoppable, instinctual.. Those two notes grind away at you—just like a shark would do. Those simple two notes written in June 1975 by the legendary John Williams frightened an entire nation off the beaches and out of the water. Without that unforgettable movie score, Stephen Spielberg's masterpiece *Jaws* could conceivably have been just another movie about a big fish.

When Spielberg first heard John's two notes, he said, "I thought he was kidding." Later he said, "I think that soundtrack was responsible for half of our ticket sales."

Iconic soundtracks, such as the one for *Jaws*, have become as memorable as the films themselves. *The Godfather, The Good the Bad and the Ugly,* and *Gone With The Wind,* are examples of powerful and unquestionably unforgettable music scores.

The day the composer artfully places his music into the middle of everyone else's vision is the day the film takes a quantum leap. That day the film truly becomes a movie. Now, imagine the excitement and anxieties of the composer.

Steve Dorff grew up in Queens, New York. At sixteen years old, he signed his first music publishing deal and went on to attend the University of Georgia. Under pressure from his parents, who knew he was a long shot to make a living writing music, he decided to become a veterinarian.

Then he met Chemistry 101.

So, Steve transitioned to a major he would never use, journalism; fortunately, he did use the university's piano rooms to continue his true passion, music.

He went on to sign a publishing contract with a company in Atlanta and, for four years wrote what Steve called "everyman music."

While in Atlanta, he met Los Angeles producer, Snuff Garrett, who invested in Steve by moving him, his wife, and his six-month-old son out to Los Angeles. Steve's son, Steven, has blossomed into a pretty fine actor in his own right, recently starring in *True Detective.*

Shortly after relocating to California, Dorf answered a frantic phone call from Snuff. He needed a song for Clint Eastwood.

"Great," Steve said. "When do you need it?"

"Tomorrow morning," Snuff said.

This was the break that Steve had been waiting for since he was a six-year-old boy in Queens, composing songs and slapping time to the windshield wipers of his dad's car.

"No problem," Steve gulped. "You'll have it."

That night over the phone with writing partner Milton Brown, the duo wrote "Every Which Way but Loose." The song was a number one hit and began Steve's five film relationship with Clint Eastwood.

Steve has gone on to write hit after hit after hit, including "Through the Years," which was sung so memorably by Kenny Rogers. In June 2018, he was inducted into the songwriters Hall of Fame in New York City.

And what's my job as a television producer?

Take a gander at the flowchart at the end of this chapter. I like to put my job into terms a layman can understand. If a television show is like a sports team, I am not the owner.

That person is the creator/executive producer, the one responsible for casting the show and the scripts. Nor am I the manager. That job is done by the director whose task it is to interpret the script and get the best performance out of the cast.

I am like the general manager.

In concert with the executive producer, everything else falls to me. Budgeting the show; hiring the staff; coordinating casting; designing, building, lighting, and dressing the sets; selecting the cameras; installing the sound equipment; scouting the locations; doing post-production and publicity—just about everything on the chart below requires my direction and input..

And my main job is to know enough about each of the department's jobs to make sure that they know they can't bullshit me.

These are just a sampling of people who work on your favorite television or movie sets. None famous, all fascinating.

The next time you go out to a movie or watch TV, hang around for the end credits and spend a few moments with some of these terrific people. They are definitely singular voices. The very least you can do is stick around to hear and recognize them.

Believe me.

They'll appreciate it.

After 60-plus hour work weeks, the craftsmen enjoy being around each other enough to play softball every fall weekend. (Courtesy of Rosario Roveto Jr.)

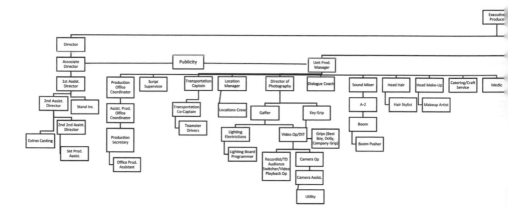

MURPHY
BROWN

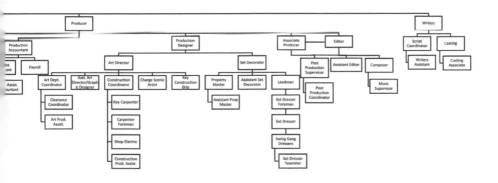

A producer is like the General Manager of a sports team. He or she has a lot of responsibility, as this chart shows. (Courtesy of Marilyn Majich)

"THE SECRET TO STAYING YOUNG IS TO LIVE HONESTLY, EAT SLOWLY, AND LIE ABOUT YOUR AGE."

– Lucille Ball

Chapter 18

THE GREATEST GENERATION

"I'm coming out to L.A.," Fran said over the phone. "I was wondering, if it's not too much of a bother, could you drive me out to Palm Springs to visit Bob Hope and President Ford."

Uh, yeah, Fran, I think I can squeeze those two into my schedule.

In her rich life, Dr. Frances Bartlett Kinne, the former president of Jacksonville University, has acquired an impressive list of friends and admirers. From Bob Hope and Jack Benny to Arthur Fiedler, Aaron Copland, Ross Perot, and Steve Forbes, corporate giants often seek her counsel. Her accomplishments are endless. So, I was delighted when she called me in the spring of 1998 concerning her visit to Southern California.

Fran first met future President Gerald Ford through her husband, Colonel Harry Kinne, a senior officer on General Douglas MacArthur's Pacific Theater staff. It was in the Pacific that Fran also met Bob Hope on one of his early USO tours. After commanding US efforts in the occupation and restoration of Germany after World War II, Colonel Kinne and Fran relocated to Jacksonville, where in 1958 Fran signed on as a part-time teacher at JU.

It was in Jacksonville where J.E. Davis, founder of the Winn-Dixie supermarket chain and his wonderful wife Flo befriended the Kinne's. J.E. Davis was Gerald Ford's fishing buddy, so the three men quickly became friends.

By 1970, Fran Kinne had become the Dean of Fine Arts at JU, the first female so designated in the country, and Gerald Ford was the Republican leader of the US House of Representatives. Seeking a college for their oldest son Jack, Gerald and Betty Ford entrusted him to Fran and JU, where the younger Ford became a casual acquaintance of mine.

Legend has it that during one break in the school year, Jack brought home a female friend from college. She got up hungry in the middle of the night and went to the kitchen, where she faced an equally hungry but buck-naked and supremely embarrassed Gerald Ford. He had totally forgotten that the Fords had a houseguest.

After driving ninety minutes from L.A., our first stop was the Bob Hope residence. Bob's 6.2-acre estate sat atop a hill overlooking the floor of the western Coachella Valley. The "hovel" was 23,366 square feet and included ten bedrooms with thirteen full or partial bathrooms. Although the desert is far from cold, the master bedroom and great room both have massive fireplaces.

The house itself resembles a volcano. The modernist structure is built of concrete and glass with an undulating copper roof that rises to an open semi-circle at its center. The home was used primarily as a second residence for the Hope family and was the place where they entertained most often, inviting friends such as Tony Bennett, Frank Sinatra, and Glen Campbell to enjoy the views.

The outside of the house had the obligatory swimming pool, a large pavilion with another fireplace, and a tennis court.

We entered his home, where an assistant showed us to the elevator. Once on the second floor, the spectacular views stole our breaths. Palm Springs and the airport appeared even more beautiful than they actually were when viewed through 360 degrees of glass. It was like being an air traffic controller inside their command center.

Before long, Bob, now in his mid-nineties, ambled in. I say ambled because he was showing his age. His sight was failing too. As he entered the room, I could swear he was humming his theme song, "Thanks for the Memories."

He greeted Fran the way only two people with more than fifty years of history can. Fran gifted Hope with Godiva chocolate. Bob eyed the box; glanced around for his wife, Dolores (who was nowhere in sight); and broke it open. "I am not supposed to have this," Bob said. "But, hell, if I won't."

He proceeded to gobble three while the two began reminiscing, telling story after story. Fran asked Bob if he remembered coming to Jacksonville University with Jack Benny in 1972.

"I'm old, not feeble." Bob cracked. "Of course, I remember."

It was the only time those two titans of show business had ever appeared on a college campus, and both gave rollicking performances. This day, Fran would try to get Hope to commit to making a return trip to Jacksonville, but Hope was having none of it.

"Oh, Bob," Fran said sweetly, accentuating her southern drawl for effect. "Jacksonville is not the end of the world, you know!"

As always, Bob would have the last succinct word. His eyes gleamed, and with that famed, sardonic smile that has delivered a million punch lines over the course of more than seven decades in show business, he glibly said, "Almost."

I almost did a spit take. His response was perfect.

With that, Fran and Bob hugged, and we said our goodbyes. We were off to see President Ford, but not before I took a photo of Fran in front of the Hope Mansion. I am told the house went on the market for $50 million upon Hope's passing at 100. Dolores lived to 102.

Fran and I were then off to our next stop, the home of the thirty-eighth president of the United States.

We arrived at a guard gate in Rancho Mirage, a Palm Springs suburb where the Fords had maintained a home office since leaving Washington, D.C., in the late '70s. I rolled down my window and announced, "Fran Kinne to see the President."

"The President is waiting for you," the guard responded, and then he honored Dr. Kinne with a crisp salute as the gate to the entrance rose in unison with his arm. I joked to Fran that I felt as if I were driving Miss Daisy.

Once inside the reception area, the president's longtime administrative assistant, Penny Circle, warmly greeted Fran. "The President is so looking forward to seeing you both," Penny said leading us toward the inner office. Fran was her normal self, bounding around handing out boxes of her trademarked Godiva chocolates to every familiar face.

Ford's home was as subtle as Hope's was ostentatious. *Palm Springs Magazine* helps jog my memories: "…Green drapes, corresponding green floral sofas, and wicker chairs sat under a geometric-patterned cedar wood ceiling. The dining room continued the color scheme with a foliage mural painted on the walls and seats with green cushions and faux bamboo legs. The only thing even vaguely Washingtonian was a tiny presidential seal on an old-fashioned telephone in the yellow-hued guest kitchen."

When we walked into President Ford's office, it opened onto a fairway of the adjacent Thunderbird Country Club. Only several yards of manicured grass separated the out-of-bounds stakes from the sliding glass doors to the left of the President's desk. Any duffer searching for a wayward drive could have just walked in.

As he rose to welcome us dressed in golf attire—short-sleeve shirt with a pullover sweater-vest and dark slacks—I was struck by just how big a man Ford was. The president reminded me some of John Wayne.

The office resembled the University of Michigan Football Hall of Fame rather than that of the thirty-eighth president of the United States. Photos of Ford's days as an MVP center for the football team and many other pieces of Michigan football memorabilia presented to the President during those years flecked the room.

I remember seeing a caricature of Egyptian President Anwar Sadat and Israeli Prime Minister Menachem Begin that the President obviously treasured. For the most part, Michigan football, photos of his beloved family, and books dominated the room. Although in his eighties, the president was still youthful and vigorous of mind.

Fran and the president warmly reminisced about mutual friends and entertained each other with stories about Bob Hope and others. By 1980, Fran had become the president of JU, only the second woman to reach that lofty position in the US.

The president reminded Fran of the honorary doctorate she had presented to him in 1984 to mark the fiftieth anniversary of the founding of Jacksonville University.

Along with the president's doctorate, Fran had commandeered the JU maintenance staff to create a "golf club" from an old length of pipe and assorted plumbing parts as a special memento. The president smiled and pointed to a corner aside one of his bookshelves where the "pipe club" proudly rested.

Before leaving, Fran asked the president if he would mind if I snapped a picture of the two of them. As badly as I wanted to take a picture with the president as well, and as sure as I was that this gentleman would have said yes, I fought the impulse.

As we headed to the door, the president stopped and put his hand on my shoulder.

"Frank, can I ask you for a favor?"

"Of course," I said, thinking what in the world could the President of the United States ask of me?

"My son Steven is an actor," he said. "Do you think there is any way you could help him get a job?"

I had to chuckle. It's a question I have been asked many times over the years. Most of the time I have a ready exit line. In fact, I knew that Steven was an actor, so I smiled, extended my hand, and said, "Mr. President, after all you did to heal this country, I'm sure that's the least I can do."

So, if you ever stumble upon *Suddenly Susan*, take note of the great performance by a handsome, blond-haired anchorman in the two-part episode, "A Tale of Two Pants." That would be Steven Ford.

Steve was always prepared, honest, amiable, and reliable. He was there when you needed him. While viewing his performance now almost twenty years later, he was even better than I had remembered him, and I liked his performance immensely then.

The same can be said of his father. Time and fresh eyes provide perspective on many things, not the least of which is the legacy of Gerald Ford.

And for Fran Kinne?

She's listed in the *Guinness Book of World Records* as the oldest college commencement speaker ever at 100 years old. Her thirty-minute commencement speech done off the top of her head without a single note received a standing ovation.

Fran passed away on Mother's Day 2020, two weeks shy of her 103rd birthday. She was a mother to all of us.

The greatest generation indeed.

Bob Hope at the Great Wall of China wearing PONY shoes. (Alamy Stock Photos)

A proud Fran and her alumni boys at JU (l-r): Artis Gilmore, Jay Thomas, Fran Kinne, and me. (Courtesy of Dr. Frances Bartlett Kinne)

GERALD R. FORD

March 27, 1998

Dear Fran:

Hope you are back in "good health." It was wonderful seeing you and Frank Pace.

Frank was most thoughtful to call his casting director on Steve's behalf. Steve really enjoyed working on the show.

Steve is now in North Carolina working on a pilot for Aaron Spelling. If it is picked up Steve will have a good part.

It's always good to see you. Thanks for the two photos. Enclosed one with my inscription and autograph.

Best regards,

Gerald R. Ford

Dr. Frances B. Kinne
4032 Mission Hills Circle, W
Jacksonville, Florida   32225

Letter from President Ford to Dr. Frances Bartlett Kinne. (Mitchell Haddad Photography)

President Gerald Ford and Fran at the 50-Year Celebration of Jacksonville University. (Courtesy of Dr. Frances B. Kinne)

"YOU ARE ONLY GIVEN A SPARK OF MADNESS. DON'T WASTE IT."

– Robin Williams

Chapter 19

JAY THOMAS –
THE KING OF THE CITY

After Jay Thomas had appeared more than twenty times on David Letterman's late-night talk show, Letterman asked his audience, "Is there a funnier man in America than Jay Thomas?"

According to the old Hollywood adage, an actor's career has four stages:

"Who the hell is Jay Thomas?"

"Get me Jay Thomas."

"Get me a young Jay Thomas."

And, finally, "Who the hell is Jay Thomas?"

The Jay Thomas I knew for almost fifty years never reached that last stage. He was always, uniquely, Jay Thomas, arguably the funniest man I have ever met.

Jon Thomas Terrell was the son of Katharine "Kathy" Guzzino, a beautiful, giddy, outspoken southern belle, and her oilman husband, Harry. Never one to let the truth get in the way of a good story, Jay's official bio read that he was raised on his mother's sprawling plantation on the banks of the Atchafalaya river in South Louisiana.

Jay's family had neither a plantation nor money. When the oil wells in Kermit, Texas, dried up, the family drifted to New Orleans. Jay's Dad died young, so his fiercely independent mom raised him and his older brother, Tim. At seventy-three, Kathy still wasn't collecting social security because she didn't want anyone to know her age.

I met Jay in the fall of 1970 when we were both students at Jacksonville University. Barely twenty years old, he had just taken over as a radio DJ at WAPE—the Big Ape. Driving though the parking lot at the Nottingham Apartments across from the university, he saw me and stopped the car.

"Do you live here?" I asked.

"Yes," he said.

"Me too. Who's your roommate?"

In college, everyone was broke and had a roommate.

"I make $19,000 a year." Jay laughed. "I don't need a roommate." With that he merrily drove off.

That was Jay.

The Big Ape billed him as "The King of The City," and indeed, he was. He was brash, bold, and uncensored and, man, was he funny.

For the next four decades, I was Robin to his Batman, Tonto to his Lone Ranger, and Pippen to his Jordan.

Jay was a fine athlete and a hell of a football player. A quarterback with one tragic flaw when the game was on the line—he threw the ball to the wrong team. Maybe he was color-blind? The year before our fraternity intramural team had an undefeated season. Jay took over and led Pi Lambda Phi to a 3-7 record.

After graduating with a sociology degree, he moved to a larger market, WAYS in Charlotte, North Carolina.

Jay said that he played quarterback for Central Piedmont Junior College *after* having graduated from JU, a four-year school. That made no sense. How could a college graduate play for a junior college team? Like I said before, facts and Jay's stories often had little in common.

Thomas was leaving the studio one night during the Vietnam War, and the newsreader told Jay that he was having trouble pronouncing Vietnamese names. Jay told the guy that whenever he saw a name he couldn't pronounce, just substitute "poontang" (slang for "pussy"). He promised no one would be any the wiser. Driving home, Jay heard the gullible jock say, "In a bloody battle in the province of, uh, Poontang, US forces killed two dozen, uh, Poontanese regulars."

Jay burned an inch of rubber off his tires speeding back to the station.

Years before shock radio, Jay's act got ballsier. He was even bolder and more uncensored in Charlotte than he had been in Jacksonville. The station plastered his face all over town on billboard-sized dollar bills, and he ran for mayor of Charlotte as "the best candidate money can buy."

Gotta lot of votes too.

He was named *Billboard* magazine's Morning Drive-Top Jock three times, but he itched to act in theater, film, and TV. His growing notoriety as a major radio talent led to a job as a morning DJ in New York City. Jay's ratings soon shot to number one, and his irreverent radio style further inspired a young Howard Stern, who was an early listener and ardent fan.

Jay's radio sidekick at the time, the inimitable Charley Steiner, later moved to ESPN to do play-by-play for the Yankees and Dodgers. My wife Karen said Jay collected people. It was a term of endearment. Jay, Charley, and I inevitably became friends for life.

As well as performing in a half dozen notable off-Broadway plays, Jay also did stand-up at the World-Famous Improv in Hell's Kitchen. His comedy exposure led to an audition for Garry Marshall's *Mork & Mindy*.

I was living in San Diego, working in advertising, when Jay called to tell me he was coming out to audition for *Mork & Mindy* in 1978. He was the brightest star on New York radio by then and had shared a large apartment, where I would crash on occasional work trips back to Manhattan. Another young co-worker of mine in San Diego also bunked with Jay when he moved to New York. He would become sportswriter and pre-eminent broadcast journalist Armen Keteyian.

Gary Marshall's *Mork & Mindy*, starring Robin Williams and Pam Dawber, was a spin-off of *Happy Days*. Mork was an alien whose spaceship crashed on earth. Stranded, he was taken in by strait-laced Mindy. Storylines revolved around Mork's attempt to understand American culture while Mindy tried to help him adjust to life on earth.

The sideshow of Robin Williams' complex personality was actually what made *Mork & Mindy* interesting. In private, Robin was quiet, introspective, and troubled. If you flung him in front of a crowd, however, he felt duty bound to perform. Sportscaster Colin Cowherd once said that Robin knew exactly what he wanted to say when he took the stage. Nothing could be further from the truth. Robin was an improvisational genius.

In *Mork & Mindy's* second season, the show replaced Mindy's dad and grandmother. Thomas was added to the cast as Remo DaVinci, a Colorado Springs deli owner. Jay immediately moved to L.A. and into an oceanfront apartment in Malibu. With the waves literally breaking under his living room, I would come up every weekend from San Diego to crash on his couch. Those weekends were usually fueled by booze and drugs. Robin felt duty bound to excel at those as well. I stuck to tequila and Jay to weed, but Robin loved the Peruvian marching powder, and money wasn't a problem.

Robin had no problem with women, either, but his main squeeze was model Patty Hanson, who later married Rolling Stone guitarist Keith Richards. It was no secret that Williams was the last person comedian John Belushi saw the night that he overdosed at the Chateau Marmont hotel on the Sunset Strip.

Jay would often joke about that on the air. "Hello, Chateau Marmont, Mr. Belushi is dead." It was never too soon for Jay.

Jay's role in *Mork & Mindy* was created to attract a younger viewing audience.

It didn't succeed.

Jay and Robin's relationship grew strained. Although they respected each other, they were never friends. Robin and Jay were so similar their humor clashed. Jay's role grew smaller and smaller, and he became more and more frustrated with each script. After only two seasons, Jay was replaced by Williams' comic idol Jonathan Winters in the role of Mork's son. Winters was almost thirty years Robin's senior. Think about the improbability of that if you will.

On Sundays during those *Mork & Mindy* years, Jay and I would go to the playground of Paul Revere Jr. High to play touch football. He'd quarterback one team while the other squad was captained by Phil Coccioletti, who dated Pam Dawber for years.

Jay called Phil the handsomest man on the planet. Roughly 6'3," Phil had quarterbacked at Appalachian State in North Carolina. Coccioletti would later introduce Jay to his future wife, New York clothing buyer Sally Michelson.

Three of the players who showed up for our pickup games each week were the Hudson Brothers, B-list celebrities at the time who had had a string of musical hits in the '70s. They parlayed their limited celebrity into a short-lived network TV series that they hosted, *The Hudson Brothers Razzle Dazzle Show.*

Bill Hudson, at the time, was married to Goldie Hawn. Bill and Goldie would bring both their children to watch the games. Kate Hudson was only four, and Oliver was in diapers. In later years, both would have success as actors, but it was fun watching them frolic on the sidelines as toddlers.

Although only playground touch football games, the Hudson brothers, complete putzes, would come dressed in full L.A. Rams uniforms.

Jay's role on *Mork & Mindy* now over, he was back to New York for another radio gig. But we had both experienced a taste of Hollywood and craved more. About this time, my career took a marked turn. Having produced at the agency for a fledgling ESPN, I left San Diego to start an L.A. production company with Jay called Pace-Thomas Productions.

Using our own money, the first concept we produced was *Super Bowl Special Memories*, hosted by Pittsburgh Steelers star Lynn Swann. The show was a series of forty-second Super Bowl vignettes bracketed by ten seconds of advertiser ID on each side—sixty seconds total.

We went to Sewickley, Pennsylvania, where my old World Football League pal John Evenson was now publicity director for the Steelers. He had arranged for us to use Pittsburgh's four Super Bowl trophies as props in our shoot. Our set was a simple, dark limbo with a spotlight on Swann and those four glistening trophies.

Apparently better producers than salesmen, we couldn't sell the show to any advertiser. The NFL listened to our pitch, viewed the final product, and although impressed, still passed. The following year, the SOBs had their own version of *Special Memories* on the air.

We learned two valuable lessons.

Don't deal with the NFL on a project that they can do better without you. More importantly, never use your own money to produce anything. We took a bath on the project but never used our own money again. In those days, taking a bath was fortunately only about $5,000 each. The lesson was well worth the tuition.

So, now for the promised Hillside Strangler story referred to in the 2nd chapter.

At the NASL finals in D.C., I met the owner of the Rochester soccer team, Charlie Schiano. Schiano was a criminal lawyer from Rochester, New York, who was representing Kenneth Bianchi. Bianchi, also from Rochester, was better known in Los Angeles as the Hillside Strangler, a serial killer who had murdered ten young women ages ten to twenty-eight and then dumped their bodies by the side of the road. A real charmer. Bianchi wanted to make a movie about his life. Jay and I decided that would be our next project.

After several face-to-face meetings in the high security prison, talks broke down. Bianchi was unwilling to admit guilt, and we were unwilling to be conned by a serial killer. We had heard in graphic detail at Bianchi's trial how he and his killing partner, cousin Angelo Bueno, had raped and tortured their victims. Jay excused himself, went to the bathroom, and violently threw up.

We were out.

The film was later made in 2003 from the point of view of the detectives who caught the murderous pair. Nick Turturro played Bueno, and C. Thomas Howell played Bianchi.

In 1981, Jay started dating a window company sales manager, Karen Huggins. Jay said, "She's wrong for me but perfect for you."

He was right. Within eighteen months, Karen and I were married.

Six years later, Karen and I attended Jay and Sally's wedding. We went on to have the same accountant, housekeeper, landscaper, and home security company. When we had our daughter, Erin, Jay quickly became her "Uncle Jay." We were so close that if I were to drown, I'm fairly certain Jay's life would pass in front of me.

Jay headed back to Los Angeles where he was hired by Power 106. There he was greeted by station-sponsored billboards and huge signs plastered to buses that screamed "WE APOLOGIZE FOR JAY THOMAS." He now commanded upward of $1 million a year.

At Power 106, Jay soon had the number-one-rated show in the market. He would knock off rival Rick Dees, becoming the first person ever to be number one in New York and later L.A.

When Jay was on a roll, I swear he could get laughs in an empty room. Jay's agent Don Buchwald, who also represents Howard Stern, had flown out from New York for the Super Bowl between the Broncos and his beloved Giants. The night before the game, a bunch of us, including Don, met up at Adriano's, a swanky little Italian joint atop Mulholland Drive overlooking Beverly Hills.

The place was bustling, and Jay was having one of his nights. Our table was making such a ruckus that I thought management was going to give us the boot. After about forty-five minutes, a large man from a silhouetted booth left the two women seated with him and lumbered in our direction. In the darkness, we couldn't see his face. I thought, oh, oh, here comes grief.

He loomed in the shadows and softly said, "Thanks for the laughter. I would have given anything to be seated at this table tonight. You really know how to live life." When he moved into the light, we all gasped. That soft-spoken gentleman was Marlon Brando.

Buchwald had negotiated into Jay's radio contract that he could still work as an actor. He was quickly cast on *Cheers*. I'll let *Cheers* executive producer Ken Levine pick up the story here in his blog:

"David Isaacs and I wrote the two-parter that introduced the character of Eddie LeBec. It actually started as just a single episode, but as the story expanded, it became clear we needed more room to tell it. A number of people read for the role, and I thought of Jay. Beyond that, there was no favoritism. The other producers were mostly unfamiliar with his work. He came in and auditioned like everyone else and won the role."

Levine went on to say:

"He was terrific in the episodes. He and Rhea made a very cute couple, so he was brought back periodically as her boyfriend. It gave us such a good story arc for Carla that we finally decided to marry them. A few episodes of recurring bliss until one day on Jay's radio show a caller asked Jay what it was like to be on *Cheers*? 'it's brutal,' he said. 'I have to kiss Rhea Perlman.'"

Well, guess who just happened to be listening?

"Jay Thomas was never seen on *Cheers* again," Levine said. "To explain his departure, we decided to just kill him, which led to one of the best episodes that David and I wrote, '*Death Takes a Holiday on Ice*.' First off, we needed a funny demise. By then, Eddie was working as a penguin in an ice show, so we decided to knock him off with a Zamboni machine accident."

Then Levine said, "We needed some comic spin for the story, and something to discredit Eddie so the audience would ultimately be glad that he was out of Carla's life. Our solution was to have Carla learn at Eddie's funeral that he was a polygamist and had a second wife who was the image of Carla. It was BIG LOVE going for big laughs. That episode got us an Emmy nomination."

In the spring of 1988, I produced my first pilot, *Murphy Brown*. Executive producer Diane English was having difficulty casting the part of Frank Fontana. I suggested Jay.

She met him and loved him so much so that she momentarily considered making the character of Frank Fontana as caustic as Jay had played him during the audition. She reconsidered though, and the part eventually went to Joe Regalbuto, who was brilliant as Frank for eleven seasons.

Diane never forgot Jay's singular voice, however, and called on him when she wrote the part of *Murphy Brown's* love interest, right-wing talk-show host Jerry Gold. Jay was nominated for an Emmy for Jerry Gold in '89 and won Emmys for the role in '90 and '91. Diane would also cast Jay as the lead in *Love & War*, which ran for three years on CBS.

Another series, *Married People*, would follow, along with star turns in feature films, including *Santa Claus 2 & 3, A Smile Like Yours, The Trails of Katie McCullough*, and *Mr. Holland's Opus*, for which I thought he should have earned an Oscar nomination as Best Supporting Actor.

He was certainly at the "Get me Jay Thomas" stage of his career.

As much success as Jay had in television and movies, it was on talk shows that he really shined. People lined up to book him. Jay was a regular guest on *Larry King, Bill Maher, Jimmy Kimmel, Sean Hannity, The View, The Today Show, Fox and Friends, Good Morning America*, MSNBC, CNN, and Fox News.

In fact, for a while Jay was the go-to liberal guest on the Fox network. Fox knew he was a sure bet to rile up their regular hosts. He was good for ratings.

It was on *The David Letterman Show*, however, that Jay became a talk-show superstar, and that wasn't by design. He saw an opportunity and threw the dice.

Typical Jay.

He always told me there was no room for any of us in show business. You have to make room for yourself. Jay certainly made that happen in 1998 when he and New York Jets quarterback Vinny Testaverde were guests on Letterman's show. A segment on the show had Testaverde and Letterman using a football to knock a meatball off a Christmas tree.

The pro football player struggled mightily to knock the meatball down, so Thomas ran out from the green room, pushed past the stage manager, grabbed a football, and threw a perfect bull's-eye on his first attempt.

An impressed Letterman invited him back every year after that, except for 2013, when Thomas had to cancel due to surgery. After every year's show, Jay would call me, delighted with his accomplishment of knocking the meatball off the tree—thankfully, there was no other team to intercept him.

One year, Letterman even held Christmas on July 4 because he couldn't wait another six months to hear what Dave called "the greatest story in late-night history."

Thomas drove David Letterman to fits every year by telling the tried-and-true tale of his misadventure with the Lone Ranger. When Jay was a radio DJ in North Carolina during the mid-70s, a local Dodge dealer hired actor Clayton Moore for a personal appearance as the Lone Ranger. It was the same character Moore had played on TV with campy brilliance for eight years.

Moore was to appear, wearing his full Carolina blue Lone Ranger outfit, replete with boots, black mask, holster, and six-shooters.

When the festivities were over, Jay and his buddy Mike Martin, a local record promoter who dressed like the rock stars he represented, snuck off behind the dumpster to get "herbed up." When they returned, whacked, they noticed that the Dodge dealer had forgotten to order a car for Moore. They offered the masked man, still in full costume, a ride back to his room at Charlotte's Red Roof Inn.

The three got stuck in heavy traffic. Frantic to escape at the nearest exit, the driver in front of them decided to back up and switch lanes. The aggravated man crashed his rear fender into Jay's car, breaking the headlight. After the collision, the older driver punched the gas pedal attempting to flee the scene. Jay, in his aging Volvo, took off in pursuit. As they weaved from lane to lane, Moore sat in the back seat, silent as a cadaver. Through his rearview mirror, Jay could see the masked man bouncing from side to side like a Bobblehead doll.

High as a giraffe's ass, they finally caught up to the speeding car.

"We finally confront the old bastard," Jay howled. "And he denies it ever happened."

The guy checked out Jay's hair, coiffed in a white man's afro, and the kaleidoscope of colors worn by Mike and decided to brazen it out.

"I never hit anybody," he screamed.

"Oh, yeah, well, I am going to call the police." Jay countered.

"Who do you think the police will believe?" The man asked. "Me or you two hippie freaks?"

With that, Clayton Moore quietly unfolded from the back seat of the Volvo in full regalia. Still wearing his mask, he placed both fists on his hips in a classic Lone Ranger pose and quietly said, "They'll believe me, citizen."

The senior citizen played his last desperate card. "I didn't know it was you," he lamented.

Every time Letterman heard this story, he squealed in delight as if he were hearing it for the first time. He would hear it often.

If you've never seen it, you truly must, and hopefully, thanks to the power of YouTube, it will remain an annual tradition.

Jay fathered two boys with Sally. A young man showed up at Jay's door one day claiming to be his son. When I suggested a paternity test, Jay said, "Forget it." One look at J.T. Harding, and you knew Jay was his father. Even their initials were the same. Jay promptly invited his new son to join his entire family at an awards dinner in Beverly Hills where Thomas was, ironically, being honored as Father of the Year. Jay and J.T. eventually became as close as he was with his other children, Jake and Sam. J.T has become a well known composer of county music songs, his work having been performed by the likes of, Kenny Chesney, Keith Urban and Blake Shelton.

So it was through the remainder of the '90s into the 2000s, until January 2013.

That month I suffered the dissected carotid, which led to the date with the Grim Reaper, which I thankfully never kept.

Jay was one of the first to come see me after I came out of intensive care. It was Super Bowl weekend in Jay's hometown of New Orleans. After he departed for the airport to attend the game, Karen said, "Jay seemed off." She asked me if I had noticed anything. I grunted, "No," but hell I wasn't noticing much of anything.

It turned out Karen was right. Jay had just come from the doctor's office, where he had just been diagnosed with throat cancer. He attributed it to eating too much pussy when he was single. Broadcasting remotely from his studio in Santa Barbara and hooked into a control room 3,000 miles away in New York, no one actually saw his decline. But for those of us who did, it was painful.

By September, he had taken a hiatus from the radio to have "an operation." By that fall, Jay should have died. He was being fed through a tube hooked into his stomach. Before specialists would allow massive doses of radiation and chemotherapy, all his teeth with fillings would have to be yanked. Jay somehow endured the pain but couldn't see anyone, not even me. Sally sent me photos of my dearest friend curled up in a fetal position, skin burned to a crisp by the radiation.

Around Thanksgiving, Jay gradually got better. He fibbed to Letterman that he wouldn't be able to appear that Christmas due to shoulder surgery but promised to return the following year. Not wanting to ruin the momentum, Letterman had John McEnroe hit tennis balls at the Christmas tree and tell the Lone Ranger story word for word as if he were Jay. By December, Jay was in remission. By January, he was back on the air. No one was any the wiser.

That lasted three years. In late November 2016, the cancer came back with a vengeance. In January 2017, I needed Jay to do an on-camera interview for my documentary *Jacksonville WHO?*, the story of Jacksonville University's rise in 1970 to become the smallest school ever to play in the NCAA Division 1 Basketball Championships. When he showed up, Jay was game as ever but losing weight. His liver was starting to shut down, and his color was changing. Jay wore glasses to cover the growing bags under his eyes but, of course, performed like the champion he was.

In June, he made his last of several recurring appearances on Showtime's *Ray Donovan*. Jay always said he'd take any job he was offered. Gaunt and frail, he showed up. Jay refused to complain or call it in. He loved to work.

By now, I was making semi-regular runs up to Jay and Sally's home in Santa Barbara to sit with him, show him the final cut of the documentary, and retell stories and lies. I am not much for telling another man "I love you," but I did exactly that in those declining days.

I said it often.

Jay would throw me out if I stayed more than ninety minutes.

"I know you," he said. "You are just like me. You were leaving before you got here."

A week or so before he passed, I called Jay and told him I had seen Mike Garrett, the former USC Heisman Trophy winner and member of the Super Bowl IV-winning Kansas City Chiefs. We had all played in a pickup football game many years before in San Diego.

Garrett made me promise to tell Jay that he was thinking of him, and that, besides George Mira, Jay had a better arm than anyone else that he had ever played with.

When I did, Jay's eyes lit up and a much-needed grin was plastered on his face.

Finally, Sally asked me and Eddie Herbert, another expatriate from New Orleans, to come up and say goodbye. It was time. Jay had passed protocol for an assisted suicide in California. It was a Sunday. On Monday he would take the medicine that would kill him.

Sally asked Eddie, a chef by trade, to prepare Jay's favorite meal. When we got there, Jay was glancing through the Sunday edition of the *New York Times*, as was his weekly ritual, ripping out clips of interest for movies that we would never make and stories that he would never tell. I will spare you the details of his appearance that day. Although heartbreaking, Jay was fearless and funny to the end. Glancing at his ninety-two-year-old mother-in-law out of earshot in the kitchen, he whispered to me and Eddie, "I can't believe that bitch is gonna outlive me."

I left knowing I would never see Jay again.

By Monday morning, Jay couldn't even swallow the medicine that could kill him.

By Wednesday, he was gone.

He was sixty-nine years old.

He would have gotten a kick out of the irony.

Sally sent out a memorial card with this message from Jay, "You would have to stay up all day and night for the rest of your life to have as much fun as I had. . . . So, when I die, don't be sad. . . . I've had a great time. I lived my entire life like I was on vacation."

Goodbye, dear friend.

I love you, pal.

Best buddies from Jacksonville University: Aleks Mihailovic, me, Jay, and Gil Vieira. (Mitchell Haddad Photography)

Jay won two Best Supporting Actor Emmys for his work as Jerry Gold in Murphy Brown. (Courtesy of Academy of Television Arts & Sciences)

With Super Bowl MVP Lynn Swann and Jay at the shooting of Super Bowl Special Memories. (Courtesy of John Evenson)

Jay, Sally, and their boys, Sam and Jake. (Courtesy of Sally Terrell)

"THE NICE THING ABOUT BE-
ING A CELEBRITY IS IF YOU
ARE BORING, PEOPLE THINK
IT'S THEIR FAULT."
— *Henry Kissinger*

Chapter 20

FAME VERSUS CELEBRITY

An internet meme of Howard Cosell with his arms around Bruce Jenner and O.J. Simpson reads, "Folks, I've just looked fifty years into the future. You're not gonna believe what I have to tell you."

America's fascination with celebrities has reached epic heights. Hell, we elected a reality TV star president. Running for president is one talent; actually doing the job is another. Although some people may have hated Hillary Clinton, we could have drawn the line at making Donald Trump president.

On TV, celebrities promote prescription drugs whose side effects "may cause death." The Kardashians' silly series garnered the highest ratings in cable television history. When Andy Warhol said, "Everyone will be famous for fifteen minutes, ' he got it wrong. He should have said everyone will be famous for five. Warhol confused fame with celebrity, commotion with accomplishment.

Honor and acclaim define fame while notoriety defines celebrity.

Barack Obama is famous; Malala is famous. Lori Loughlin is a celebrity; the musical group BTS are celebrities. Monica Lewinsky was infamous but still a celebrity.

Get the difference?

Celebrity is like a David Blaine illusion. Maybe it seems real, but perception shouldn't be confused with reality. Sort of like those diamond-like trinkets Joan Rivers used to sell on the Home Shopping Network.

Some celebrities are famous, like Tiger Woods and Bruce Springsteen. They are accomplished people who also court and embrace the limelight. That's the catch with celebrity and those who buy into it. It's a full-time job, one that needs to be fed and nurtured. To many, it is like a drug coursing through their veins. Like any addiction, the need for it often becomes all-consuming.

Many who have fame thrust upon them are never comfortable with its accompanying demands. Ultimately, they learn to grudgingly coexist with it, or like Greta Garbo and J.D. Salinger, they withdraw completely.

For others it's a curse. All Charles Lindbergh ever wanted to do was fly an airplane across the Atlantic. Fame would cost him a son.

Bob Dylan ran away from fame to Woodstock. He didn't want to be a spokesperson for a generation. He just wanted to make music.

In July 1969, Buzz Aldrin became famous when he walked on the moon. In the ensuing forty months, ten other men would follow in his footsteps. In the years after their return to earth, Aldrin and most of the others underwent uncommon depression. I once asked Aldrin over dinner why so many of the "moon men" had suffered so many personal problems. "It's simple," he said. "NASA prepared us for everything that could happen on our way to the moon but for nothing that would happen when we got home."

In short, they could not deal with the celebrity that fame brought with it.

Don't kid yourself. It wasn't drugs that killed Elvis some forty years ago. Celebrity consumed Elvis, Amy Winehouse, and Nipsey Hustle too.

Fame is also fickle. Disrespect it, and it can break you as quick as make you. Pete Rose, Mike Tyson, Bill Cosby and Bill Clinton thought fame entitled them to play by different rules. They thought their fame would protect them. Instead it brought them shame. Hall of Fame basketball player Charles Barkley once said, "I ain't nobody's role model." Barkley was lambasted for the statement, but the truth is he was right. The same goes for hero worship.

Some years ago, I ran into Bruce Jenner at Musso & Frank Grill a legendary Hollywood watering hole supposedly still frequented by the ghosts of past patrons Humphry Bogart and Errol Flynn. I was surprised and saddened by Jenner's appearance.

Plastic surgery had transformed him into some kind of porcelain-looking freak. It was a desperate attempt by Jenner to stay youthful-looking and maintain whatever tenuous hold that celebrity still accorded him. And he was still a man then. Little could I have guessed the sordid celebrity play that he starred in behind his sad facade.

If Bogey's ghost still haunts Musso & Frank Grill and he had to repeat his famous line, "Of all the gin joints in all the world, she has to walk into mine." Jenner's appearance would have forced him to change his pronoun.

People often ask me about Brooke Shields and Andre Agassi, two extraordinary people whom I am very fond of. While Brooke loves being a celebrity and the limelight that goes with fame, Andre hates it. Given the choice of attending a gala Hollywood premiere or spending a quiet night at home, Brooke would pick the gala and Andre, undoubtedly, the night at home.

That was possibly one of the reasons for their breakup. Opposites attract, but passion wanes. Caroline Kennedy rarely appeared in public, but the late John Jr. was on *Murphy Brown*. It doesn't make one person right or the other wrong. Living in a fishbowl just forces you to make choices.

I've been around famous people and celebrities my entire adult life. From John Wayne and Frank Sinatra to Sabrina Carpenter and Zendaya. I've been with some on their way up, many at the height of their fame and celebrity, and others after their star has faded. One thing I can tell you is that almost unanimously, they really have no interest in being anyone's role models.

So, why do you care? Why would you care if Ben dumped Jennifer Garner or Jennifer dumped Ben? Why do you care that Jennifer Lopez divorced her second husband after ten minutes and is now engaged to Alex Rodriguez? Have you ever seen two bigger celebrity whores?

Celebrities becoming politicians began when George Murphy, an actor in the '30s, was elected senator in California. It led to Ronald Reagan being elected governor then president. Jesse "freaking" Ventura was elected governor of Minnesota. Finally, Donald Trump of all people, the host of *The Apprentice* and *Celebrity Apprentice*, was given the keys to the White House. Imagine that. In a turnabout of fair play, he will probably turn the Oval Office into a series, *Acting President.*

Don't be enticed by fame or celebrity. Don't buy a reverse mortgage just because some company paid Tom Selleck to tell you he did his homework on them. Honestly Tom, how much money do you need?

I remember my parents' generation being seduced to smoke cigarettes by the macho image of the Marlboro Man. He was the guy every woman wanted and every man wanted to be. Well, thanks to those cigarettes, the actor who portrayed the Marlboro Man died a slow, agonizing death from cancer, as did many of that generation. Today cigarette ads are banned from TV, and the networks forbid us from even allowing an actor to light up on camera.

Remember this about celebrity; it's like poison. It can't hurt you if you don't swallow it.

Secretary Hillary Clinton, pictured with Murphy Brown director Pamela Fryman, was inordinately famous. Still, she lost the 2016 Presidential election to a celebrity, Donald Trump. (Courtesy of Pamela Fryman)

"I HAVE FOUND THAT YOU DON'T NEED TO WEAR A NECKTIE IF YOU CAN HIT."

– Ted Williams

Chapter 21

ONE MAGICAL YEAR

It was a perfect night early in November 2018, and my daughter Erin was on the studio lot to marry Charlie, the man she loved. The room was packed with happy friends and family. My eyes lingered a few moments on an unlikely pair sharing one of the seamlessly set black-and-white tables.

One of the men took a white handkerchief from the pocket of his black tuxedo and gently rubbed it across his forehead, as if he were smoothing the wrinkles out of it. That man, all six feet of him, would have been more comfortable in cleats, a form-fitting uniform, and a peaked hat. He was the winner of seven American League batting titles, so many in fact that the league went and named their award after him.

The other man sitting directly across from him was of similar height, wore his gray hair cropped like a drill sergeant, and probably would have been more comfortable wearing Shakespearean tights or camouflage fatigues. He had also proved himself a master of his craft, not in baseball but as a Tony award-nominated actor, a bona fide movie star, and a playwright to boot.

The two had met because the gray-haired fellow had starred in a movie that we made nearly three decades earlier about the greatest baseball player who ever lived, *Babe Ruth*. The playing field and their height were not the only things they had in common. Both had gone through the pain, the discipline, and the sacrifice necessary for paragons to excel. Simply put, they prepared with all they had, and they never gave less than the 100 percent demanded of them.

The sun had barely broken the eastern sky that January morning in 1991, and Rod Carew seemingly had every reason to be nervous.

Any minute now, the call delivering the verdict would come from Jack Lang, secretary of the Baseball Writers of America.

Rod kept telling himself and anyone else who would listen that he had probably pissed off so many writers there was no way he'd get into the Baseball Hall of Fame on the first ballot. To receive that exclusive honor from baseball's shrine at Cooperstown, New York, a vote of 75 percent of the electorate would be necessary.

Remember baseball, hell, life itself, was different in the twentieth century. Even such baseball giants as Joe DiMaggio, Yogi Berra, Cy Young, Jimmie Foxx, and Whitey Ford had been denied entrance in their first year of eligibility. It was not until 2019 that a player, Mariano Rivera, would be voted in with 100 percent of the ballots, and believe me, Rivera was no better than those legends.

Rod wasn't really as nervous as the front he put on; otherwise, he never would have assembled a host of family and friends at the Rod Carew Baseball Academy in Placentia, California, nor would he have seated himself in front of the oversized blowup of a 1977 *Time* magazine cover proclaiming him, "Baseball's Best Hitter." When it came to his hitting ability, Rod was both a secure and proven commodity.

When Jack's call came, Rod got the credit he had earned. Carew had been elected into the Hall of Fame as only the twenty-second man in baseball history to do so on the first ballot. He had been rewarded with almost 91% of the vote, which meant he had pissed off only 9% of the baseball writers.

The following month, I received a call from Larry Lyttle, who had just swapped his longtime position as the second in command at Warner Bros. Television for an independent production deal with the studio. I had known Larry through my series work at Warners, and he knew all about my baseball background and my friendship with Rod.

He had just sold his script for a *Babe Ruth* movie to his good friend and weekend softball teammate, the legendary president of NBC Brandon Tartikoff.

"Would you produce the movie?" he asked.

Even though Larry and I were friends, neither he nor I had ever produced a full-length movie, so I found myself seriously surprised yet flattered.

"Papazian [Warner's vice president] said you're my guy, so, you're my guy," said Larry

"Hell, yes I will do it."

I would have done it for free.

Later that February, while the finishing touches were being put on the script, I got a call from Dan O'Dowd, then assistant general manager of the Cleveland Indians, asking if Rod would be interested in joining the team as a spring training instructor.

When I told Rod about Dan's inquiry, he immediately placed a call to ex-Angels teammate and future Colorado manager Don Baylor, another former MVP. Baylor gave Rod a piece of advice: "Try it but be aware that these kids are a lot different than when we played."

Rod was itching to get back into baseball, but because of his forced retirement in '86, relations had soured with his two former teams, the Twins and Angels, so Cleveland's offer was both interesting and gratifying.

I told Dan that Rod was in.

He was to report to the Indians training camp in Scottsdale, Arizona, in early March. Once he arrived for work, Rod reveled in tutoring the many talented young Cleveland hitters, such as Sandy Alomar Jr., Manny Ramirez, and future Hall of Famers Roberto Alomar and Jim Thome.

Meanwhile back in Hollywood, casting had started for our film, *Babe Ruth*. It would continue into June when the movie began shooting. We had whittled our choices down to actors Clancy Brown or Stephen Lang for Babe, Bruce Weitz or Joel Grey for Miller Huggins, and Neal McDonough or Mathew Glave for Lou Gehrig.

In the process, we had also auditioned the actress Rita Wilson for Clare. She had become Mrs. Tom Hanks only three years prior and would have been a more recognizable name, but the part ended up going to Lisa Zane.

Clancy Brown was physically more suited to play Babe, but there was something indefinable about Stephen Lang. We had seen him in the series *Crime Stories* and in smaller but critically acclaimed movies, such as *Last Exit to Brooklyn* and *Band of the Hand*, but an intangible element that he had exhibited in his performance in the television drama *Death of a Salesman* kept bringing us back.

Stephen had co-starred with Dustin Hoffman and John Malkovich in that marvelous production. Something below the surface convinced us that he was our guy. We had spotted an inherently vulnerable trait in Lang that we had not seen in Clancy, who had traces of a harder edge.

Our Babe would need that sensitivity; plus, Lang was so damned personable, another trait needed to successfully play the legendary Bambino. Hell, Secretariat was "The Babe Ruth of Horses." Michael Jordan was "The Babe Ruth of Basketball." Don Rickles was "The Babe Ruth of Comedy." We needed a Babe who was larger-than-life. We decided to go with Lang.

Weitz over Joel Grey should have been a no-brainer in favor of the *Hill Street Blues* star, but there was a quality about Joel Grey that Larry Lyttle, director Mark Tinker, casting maven John Levey, and I kept coming back to.

We tried to convince ourselves that our audience could get past Joel's magnificent Academy Award-winning performance as the effete emcee in director Bob Fosse's movie *Cabaret,* but in the end, we couldn't. The role went to Bruce. Good thing, too, because in the words of the *L.A. Times*'s Jim Murray, "Bruce Weitz almost stole the show as Miller Huggins."

Our last big role, that of Lou Gehrig, came down to two really fine young actors. The part went to Neal McDonough, who had played baseball at Syracuse and had his SAG card, over Mathew Glave, who did not have that cherished card. We didn't want to trust such a big part to a first-time actor, even one as fine as Glave. We did cast Glave in a smaller part; thus, he got his SAG card. Both he and McDonough have gone on to have long and notable careers.

While we were casting, Rod was wrapping up spring training. Together we planned a trip to Cooperstown, a scouting trip of sorts, to see the museum. Lord knows we would have no time for such luxuries during induction time in late July, so I stopped by Scottsdale to pick up Rod.

There I spotted a middle-aged little person named Cy Buynak, who was the longtime, visiting clubhouse manager for the Indians. I remembered Babe's Yankees had a little person as a bat boy named Eddie Bennett. Captain Obvious smacked me right across the mug. I marched over, introduced myself, and hired him on the spot to play Eddie.

I didn't really have the authority to hire Cy, but I knew Larry would be okay with it. Lyttle gave me a lot of leeway on this movie, more than most producers often get on a film. For that I was thankful, as I was for many of his decisions. Larry would make a lot of right calls. Lyttle went on to become a millionaire several times over when he created and produced the show *Judge Judy*, which at the time of this writing is still running original episodes.

We still had to lock in a location for the Yankee Stadium scenes. It came down to Milwaukee County Stadium or Cleveland Municipal Stadium. Like Yankee Stadium, both were designed by Osborne Engineering of Cleveland. Yankee Stadium was out because the old stadium had been changed too much in the mid-'70s reconstruction.

Larry, Tinker, and I made a trip to both cities and decided that Cleveland would double for Yankee Stadium. With Cleveland, our production designer could do more to make the outfield walls look the way New York's appeared during the Babe's era. Additionally, that city looked more like Manhattan in the '20s and '30s than Milwaukee did.

Cy was thrilled with the choice and knowing Dan O'Dowd would make my job immeasurably easier with the Indians. Everything was falling into place. The non-Yankee Stadium stuff would be shot in an old minor league stadium in Ontario, California.

Lang was a pretty good athlete, but he only weighed 175 pounds and hit from the right side. When Gary Cooper played Lou Gehrig in *Pride of the Yankees,* the producers flipped the negative so Cooper could hit right-handed but appear left-handed. To do that, we would have to reverse all the logos and printed signs on anything that you could read. Our film did not have the time nor the money to do that.

Lang immediately started adding weight and eventually gained 25 pounds. A more formidable task for Lang would be transforming his image into the powerful, left-handed-hitting Sultan of Swat. I enlisted Rod to make the task easier. Lang would have as technically sound a hitting instructor as anyone could ever hope for.

The first day of training, Lang showed up to Rod's Hitting Academy five minutes late. He had a forty-five-minute drive from L.A. A native New Yorker, Lang hadn't left himself enough time.

Rod told Stephen if he was ever late again, he needn't bother to show up.

Lang was mortified.

Instead of pulling what many actors would have pulled, saying "I don't need this shit," Stephen threw himself into the task, hitting four times a week with Rod. He swung that lumber until his hands bled. Rod recognized that Stephen's work ethic commanded the same commitment to detail that had driven him his whole career.

A bond was formed.

That spring Rod was named honorary captain of the AL All-Stars, opposite Hank Aaron, the honorary captain of the National League. In the meantime, I received a call from Major League Baseball informing me that Rod and Hank had been invited to the White House to meet President George H.W. Bush. I relayed the message to Rod but not completely. I simply told him the president wanted to meet him.

"Is the president coming to Los Angeles?" Rod asked.

Even though Rod and I had become as close as fingers on a glove, I couldn't believe my ears.

"No. Of course not," I said.

"Then why would I want to go to the White House? I have already been to the White House and met two presidents."

Even though he said no, that sentence made me grin like a gorilla who had just seen his reflection in the mirror.

What a ball-breaker.

"Is the president coming to Los Angeles?"

The one-liner was so good that we wrote it into the script for *Babe Ruth*: "Is the president coming to New York?"

We started shooting first in California and then moved on to Cleveland.

We had signed a deal with Major League Baseball to utilize the names and logos of the New York Yankees. In a major public relations coup, we cast Pete Rose as Ty Cobb. This set off a major brouhaha because Pete had been banned from the game in 1988 for betting on baseball.

Remember, we had a binding contract with the Yankees. Their logo was set in stone, but we hadn't closed the deal for any other team uniforms yet. MLB refused to sign any deal if Pete Rose remained in the movie.

Larry would not budge. Pete was going to be in our movie. MLB stayed resolute about Pete not wearing a uniform. They were angling for us to take Rose out of the movie and were using the unsigned uniform deal as leverage.

Larry still wouldn't budge. He wanted Pete.

Instead of taking him out of the picture, Larry resourcefully told us to build a hotel room in the bowels of Cleveland Municipal Stadium. We would shoot the Ty Cobb scenes there.

No one was any the wiser.

As for the uniforms, we said "screw you" to MLB on that too. Rather than using the team nicknames on the uniforms, we went with the generic city names Boston, Detroit, and Chicago in block letters, which in the '20s and '30s were how the away uniforms looked anyway.

The shoot went great.

Pete was great.

And Lang?

Lang was phenomenal.

Just in case, Rod was on site in California keeping an eye on his protégé.

Noted author Robert Creamer, whose book *Babe: The Legend Comes to Life* was partially the basis for the movie, showed up on the set to write a story for *Sports Illustrated*.

When Creamer saw the results of Lang and Carew's collaboration he wrote, "We came out onto the field near third base, and beyond a big, camera crane, I could see a pitcher throwing to a catcher, an umpire behind him and a white-shirted crowd cheering. And, my God, there was Babe Ruth at bat! I swear, that was my reaction: There's Babe Ruth!"

To read Creamer's story, you can go to: https://www.si.com/vault/1991/09/30/125014/the-babe-goes-hollywood-the-bambinos-biographer-visited-the-set-of-a-television-movie-to-see-the-legend-come-to-life

Now that filming was complete and the editor had all the footage, our attention turned full-time to the All-Star Game. Then to Cooperstown for Rod's induction.

The first thing I had to do was write him a speech.

That was easy. We talked about the essence of what he wanted to communicate. Then I added my own love of the game's history to give Rod's speech a little more color. Now all Rod had to do was learn it.

On our pre-dawn flight to Toronto, I recognized Otis Williams, the deep-voiced bass singer from the Temptations, coming on to our plane. Following closely behind were the other members of the most famous male singing group of the '60s and '70s. Ever alert to such things, I awoke Rod who, as was his custom on airplanes, had fallen asleep already.

As soon as the plane reached cruising altitude of 10,000 feet, Rod unclicked his seatbelt and went over to see Otis. Of course, he knew Otis. Who didn't he know? He had left game tickets for the Temps several times on their tour stops in Minnesota. The next night, Rod, my wife Karen, and I were ringside for the Temptations concert in Toronto, singing along to tunes the likes of "My Girl," "Since I Lost My Baby," and "Ain't Too Proud to Beg."

Not too proud to beg themselves, the Angels offered Rod a uniform to wear to the All-Star Game the next day. The Twins did also. Rod crossed them both up. At home plate next to Ted Williams, Joe DiMaggio, and Henry Aaron, Rod Carew wore a Cleveland Indians uniform.

"I don't work for the Twins or the Angels." With his ego still bruised from forced departures from both teams in '86, he said, "I work for the Indians and will wear their uniform proudly."

The Indians had been dreadful up through the '80s and into the early '90s. So bad in fact that Hollywood made a movie about their ineptitude, *Major League*. They were the worst draw in the American League in 1991, averaging an attendance of only 12,828 that year.

Still, as I said before, those Indians had a good core of young players who went on to play in two World Series in the '90s and sell out 480 consecutive dates during that run.

One of their young catchers, Sandy Alomar Jr., said that the players were shocked to see Rod wearing the Indians uniform that night. The mere fact that he was proud to showcase the Indians at such a high-profile venue "made us proud to be Indians." For some, it was a turning point.

Walking back to the hotel after the game, Rod said, "Oh, did I tell you we had a visitor before the game?"

"Who?" I asked.

He smiled a self-satisfied smirk. "President Bush, and the first guy he made a beeline to was me. And you wanted me to go to Washington?"

After which, he pulled out a blue velour box and presented me with his All-Star ring. To this day, I'm very proud of that gift.

We arrived in the quaint, little town of Cooperstown in upstate New York a couple of days early. The Clark Family knew what they were doing in the '30s when they decided to locate the Hall of Fame in Cooperstown, which is nestled between bucolic lakes. Without that iconic structure, I doubt tens of thousands of people would streak to that town each summer merely to visit the birthplace of James Fenimore Cooper.

It was a good thing we had done our sightseeing in the spring. Rod was too busy to venture out of the hotel other than to attend an evening celebratory party or two. When he wasn't practicing his speech, he was signing baseballs, bats, and photographs to fulfill a massive contract with Home Shopping Network.

That year we tripled the number of signings and appearances we made.

Induction day was magical. Willie Mays, Hank Aaron, Joe DiMaggio, Stan Musial, Ted Williams, Mickey Mantle, and Sandy Koufax were all there. Stephen Lang also came to honor Rod. My Mom and Dad were there, too, along with Karen and our young daughter, Erin.

Quick story aside, the Otesaga Hotel was off-limits to everyone but Hall of Famers and their guests. My dad was star struck walking the hallways with all his baseball heroes. He took polaroids with Joe D., Ted Williams, Yogi Berra, and Pee Wee Reese. He had them all autographed too—except for Pee Wee. He thought that I wouldn't recognize that he had forged Pee Wee's signature, but the P in Pee Wee was too similar to the distinctive P in Pace that I had counterfeited so many times in high school. I quickly busted him for that one.

Mom and Dad were taken by Stephen as well.

Turns out Lang lived in the same town of North Castle, New York as they did. Babe Ruth's ninety-year-old daughter Julia was there too. She marveled at the photos of Stephen from the movie and the transformation he had made into the man she simply called "Daddy."

The day was magical. En route to the podium, Mr. Cub, Ernie Banks, shouted out, "Keep it short, Rook," which relaxed Rod. His speech was flawless.

To view Rod's speech, go to:
https://www.youtube.com/watch?v=uaE_TqYxUHA

The close of his speech was especially powerful when Rod called up memories of baseball's historical figures. So powerful that in 2011, I asked Rod if I could rewrite some elements of his closing lines for Artis Gilmore's Naismith Memorial Basketball Hall of Fame speech.

Of course, Rodney, being a friend of the Big Fella, said yes.

From there, it was back to complete the editing of *Babe Ruth*.

The movie premiered on NBC during the World Series and received great reviews, especially Stephen's portrayal of Babe. Rod got numerous accolades for his work with Stephen, but even Rod will tell you that he had a hard-working student. Topps even produced a series of *Babe Ruth* movie baseball cards to promote the film, which would win an Emmy in 1992.

Through the years, Rod and Stephen would stay close. Rod would ask how Steve was doing and rush out to see *Tombstone, Don't Breathe, Gettysburg, Gods and Generals, Avatar* or whatever film Stephen was in.

Stephen would drop me a note and just ask for "himself." That's how he referred to Rodney as "himself." It was always the student and the teacher with them. Like Coach Wooden in basketball, Rod reveled in being a teacher.

When Rod was having his heart problems, Steve was amongst the first to call and did so several times throughout the ordeal. Each time they saw each other, no matter how many years went by, it was indeed a happy reunion.

So, there they were at my daughter Erin's wedding, sitting together with their wives, Tina and Rhonda. Steve and Tina had interrupted their national tour of Lang's one-man show *Beyond Glory* to make the trip in from Florida. All because of an enduring friendship that had started in 1991 and for that little girl that they had both watched grow into a woman, our daughter, Erin.

Lang was on time too. In fact, he beat Rod there.

Carew had taught him well. His teacher was pleased.

Rhonda and Rod Carew captured during a serene moment in Cooperstown, New York. (Courtesy of The Baseball Hall of Fame and Museum)

Stephen Lang as Babe Ruth. Pete Rose as Ty Cobb. (PF Collection)

At Erin and Charlie's wedding, buddies Rod Carew and Stephen Lang with Apollo 15 Commander David Scott. Scott, on July 31, 1971, was the first man to drive on the Moon. (Gregory Ross Photography)

"IF YOU CAN'T RIDE TWO HORSES AT ONCE, YOU SHOULD GET OUT OF THE CIRCUS."

— Asking Alexandria

Chapter 22

THE GOLDEN RULE

So back to that perfect night I spoke of in the last chapter.

My daughter had just married a terrific guy named Charlie Moore and just like that was Erin Moore.

She had always told my wife Karen and I that she wanted to get married on the Warner Bros. lot where she had grown up. So, that's where we did it, right on the very same streets Audrey Hepburn had filmed *Wait Until Dark*, Robert Preston had led *The Music Man's* seventy-six trombones, and George Clooney had become the new generation's Cary Grant on *ER*.

As the night raced by, my mind was filled with so many thoughts, not the least of which was the wonderment of how our daughter had grown up so quickly. I also drifted reflectively on the many good times I had cherished at this studio.

I'd been in this business more than forty years. I had met giants so modest that they attribute their success to luck and talentless people so full of themselves that they strut sitting down.

I'd like to think that I was somewhere in between.

One rule will absolutely guarantee a successful career in show business. Unfortunately, no one seems to know what that rule is. As a producer of more than 700 television episodes and three movies, let me share my ironclad formula for success.

Hire the best people. Let them do their damn jobs and pray for luck. Any person who does not in part attribute their success to luck is a liar.

The first question I asked myself before writing this book was who the hell would want to read a book about me? The answer was painfully obvious.

No one.

So, I didn't write this book about me. I wrote it about the people whom I've been lucky enough to meet along the way and about a philosophy of life that has paid me ridiculous dividends. It's simple. I have a talent for remembering unique voices. Once I hear one, I rarely sever the connection. I never let people pass through my life. If you make a friend in high school or college, why isn't that person a friend forever?

No matter a person's lot in life, I always observed the Golden Rule. I wouldn't presume to judge a janitor any more than I would put an athlete or actor on a pedestal. I treated people the way I like to be treated and refused to be intimidated by either fame or fortune. Using those guidelines, I've been fortunate enough to nurture many lasting friendships.

Growing up only a few miles from New York City enabled me to interact with a variety of personalities from every ethnic background. The values of color-blindness and tolerance for all religions, which I developed on the sandlots and blacktops, served me only too well in later years.

As common as concrete on eastern streets is a form of verbal jujitsu. If I don't know you or am meeting you for the first time, I'm going to be polite, amiable, and accommodating. If we're friends or I like you a lot, I'm going to break your balls and expect the same in return.

Vinny was one of my buddies in the old neighborhood. He had teeth as white as a nun's habit. We called him "Chicklets." Wally had big ears. All us kids called him "Wingnut." When I was ten years old, Richard moved next door to me. He told all us kids that he didn't like to be called "Dick." To this day, sixty years later, we still call him "Cock."

The guys we nicknamed weren't pissed, just the opposite. It gave them an identity and made us all even closer.

It's a New York thing. We just love to break each other's balls.

Hell, even Joe DiMaggio's nickname with the Yankees was "Dago." Times change.

It's the way things were in the old neighborhood. We went along to get along and got along to survive. You know the kind of guy who everyone likes as soon as they meet him? That's not me. I have been described as an acquired taste.

Ego will kill you in this business. Some producers have a few hits and then stroll down lover's lane holding their own hand. Not me.

That's not how I operated. I never thought I knew it all. I just worked as hard as I could, took advantage of any breaks thrown my way, and never let a swelled head interfere with my decisions.

In a pretentious world of glitter, make-believe and fealty, maybe I've been successful because I've always stayed true to who I was and where I came from. Whether consciously or unconsciously, I stayed real. Perhaps the irreverence and social flexibility that I practiced in the old neighborhood allowed celebrities whom I'd meet for the first time to recognize something different in me.

A lot of my pals growing up didn't have the benefit of a formal education. Some didn't have the money or the opportunity to go to college. Instead, they possessed an intangible that us kids liked to call "street smarts." They learned how to create their own breaks, think fast, and recognize an opportunity.

The key to success in this business is not trying to impress people with how much you think you know but by listening, learning, cultivating, and maintaining relationships. I learned early to stay humble and listen to what the people I hired had to say.

I've watched young arrogant actors walk away from lucrative contracts because they felt the work was beneath them, only to end up soon after on the junk heap of obscurity. Good judgment comes from experience, and let's face it, a lot of experience unfortunately comes from bad judgment.

I endeavored to make this book not a work of art but the story of a life's work driven by art.

I tried to chronicle the world of entertainment and sports and shine a spotlight on those rare characters whose exuberance for life transcended the medium and eventually penetrated our everyday consciousness so deeply that they made indelible imprints on American culture—those unique personalities who drove the creative process and created show business magic.

I wanted this to be a vocation-based narrative occasionally drifting to my family, my friends, and the lessons that I have learned from a lifetime in film, journalism, and sports.

My beloved mother used to shout, "Turn off that TV. You'll never make a living in sports or television. Go to work." Well, I never really turned off that TV, but I did start delivering newspapers at twelve-years-old, and fifty-eight years later, I still haven't stopped working.

When I first graduated from Jacksonville University, I made a quick stop home to New York for Christmas with my parents and brothers Bruce and Douglas, before heading to L.A. to seize an opportunity to work as a public relations man for the World Football League. What a crapshoot those two years were.

The first year that I was in Portland I watched Marty Schottenheimer start the morning as a linebacker and finish the afternoon as the teams' linebacker coach. It was the beginning of a legendary coaching career for Marty, one which would see him finish as the 8th most winningest coach in NFL history.. A year later, I found myself working with the Chicago Winds and an ownership group whom I'll charitably describe as "deese, dems, and dose" guys.

Four of these owners wouldn't even allow me to take their photos for the media guide. One member of the group had a temper so bad that I secretly nicknamed him Tony Tourettes. What a character. He could have started a fight in an empty room. When mob boss Sam Giancana was murdered, I didn't see those same four owners for weeks. My suspicions of "wise guys" were confirmed, wild times indeed.

When the World Football League folded after two years, I dove headfirst into advertising.

I started working for a small company in San Diego. The Phillips Organisation Ltd specialized in sports and sporting good products. It was with that small successful advertising company in San Diego, under the direction of Bob Phillips, that my life changed dramatically. In 1979, a visionary named Bill Rasmussen walked into my little office and started me on a totally different career path.

His vision and flexibility and, again, that singular voice spurred him to throw the dice. Recognizing a unique opportunity, he started a new network called ESPN.

He needed content to fill airtime and went on to tell me that his new Entertainment and Sports Programming Network would give me all the programming time I could handle if my advertising client, Ektelon, would put up the money to produce a national racquetball championship. Needless to say, I said yes. Just like that, I was a producer.

For five years, ESPN ran the Ektelon Natural Light racquetball championships, alongside such obscure sports as Australian rules football and Irish hurling. I honed my chops, worked hard, and watched Rasmussen's network explode.

By no small coincidence, Dave Gavitt formed the Big East Conference the same year that ESPN started in a small trailer in upstate Connecticut. The colorful personalities of regional college basketball coaches Rollie Massimino, John Thompson, and Louie Carnesecca helped ESPN blow up into the national network that it is today.

In my four decades as a producer, I've worked with them all, from Jennifer Aniston to Zendaya—or, as I often say with tongue planted firmly in cheek, "all of them from A to Z." I am the ultimate sidekick, Tonto to their Lone Ranger, Robin to their Batman.

My relationships with all of them and my friendships with some of them has reinforced a tenet that I have believed in all my life. A man's proudest accomplishments can't be measured in money.

Tennis great Andre Agassi once told me that he admired his then-wife Brooke Shields because her product is prejudiced. Andre could not work like that. His results can't be disputed. The final score is right up there on the scoreboard in black and white.

I once produced a television pilot based on the play *Driving Miss Daisy* with Dame Joan Plowright. Alfred Uhry wrote the masterpiece, and it won the Pulitzer Prize. Alfred teamed up with Richard Zanuck to produce the movie, which won four Academy Awards.

Uhry and Zanuck teamed with me and *ER* and *The West Wing's* executive producer/head writer John Wells to produce the TV adaptation of *Driving Miss Daisy*. It was the best half hour of television I was ever involved with, yet it never even made the cut for series consideration. TV is a tough racket. Don't ever think otherwise.

The public's taste is unpredictable, yet we producers are forced to depend on viewers' subjective decisions to determine if we're successful at our jobs. That's one of the things I love about sports.

I'd like to think the reader took away from this book a no-holds-barred tale of a man who has done things he's proud of and some things that he's not so proud of. A man who along the way was truly grateful that he's never done anything that he's ashamed of.

Maybe that's how the good Lord keeps score. Who knows?

I hope that when the third act is over, and the curtain comes down that I can leave behind a legacy of kindness. Enough goodwill that no man can ever judge my life subjectively. Successful husband, father, and producer make for a splendid epithet, but a fair and kind man is almost as good. When all is said and done, I'd like to be remembered as a person who helped make people's dreams come true, and in return those same people made my dreams come true.

I want everyone who took the time to read this missive not to have to question how it all turned out. I want them to see the results. I want that final score marked in black and white, in plain sight, right up there on the scoreboard.

Erin and Charlie's wedding day on the steps of the courthouse at Warner Brothers Studios, Burbank, California. (Gregory Ross Photography)

ACKNOWLEDGMENTS

This memoir is based on Frank Pace's personal experience and provides a firsthand account of his involvement in the sports and entertainment industries.

These behind-the-scenes incidents are portrayed to the best of Pace's memory and are not intended to cause malice, to harm, or to embarrass.

Rather, the author has retold them in his own way to evoke the feeling and meaning of what was said. In all instances, the essence of the dialogue is accurate.

In three instances, the authors quoted verbatim from other sources. In the Jay Thomas chapter, a section was reprinted from writer Ken Levine's blog. We knew the story but could not retell it as accurately as someone who was there.

In the George Lopez chapter, the Pebble Beach story was bylined by George, but every word was ghosted by Frank Pace. Although it appeared in a 2005 issue of *Sports Illustrated*, George Lopez approved our use of the story.

In the Gerald Ford and Bob Hope chapters, some of the elements of the Ford family's interior design and the Hope home were based in part on a March 2012 issue of Palm Springs life.

The authors would like to acknowledge our agent Julia Lord of Lord Literary Management in New York City. Richard Stayton, who edited our first draft, and Shirley Rash who edited the final draft. Alex Poli, who designed both the front and back covers. Brooke Shields, who graciously provided us with the foreword. Diane English, Rod Carew, George Lopez and Armen Keteyian, who wrote the back-cover testimonials.

Thanks as well to Douglas Sikes, Randy Baumgardner, and everyone at Acclaim Press who made this all possible. To Kelly Sinner Biggins for her legal counsel. To Tim Mead, president of the Baseball Hall of Fame. To T.J. Simers for helping me get this off the ground. To Fran Kinne for her inspiration. To Jennifer O'Connor for working with two dinosaurs to bring their computer skills into the twenty-first century. To Tom and Cathy Brock for their advice and editing diligence. To, last and not least, all the casts, crews, staffs and sports teams that we have worked with these last forty plus years.

It was worth it all. Madeleine Frances "Frankie" Moore, born February 10, 2020. (Courtesy of Erin and Charlie Moore)

ABOUT THE AUTHORS

Frank Pace

A four-time Emmy Award nominee, Frank Pace has produced more than 700 hours of network television in a career that has spanned nearly four decades. His credits include *Head of the Class, Suddenly Susan, George Lopez, Shake it Up, Girl Meets World,* and *Murphy Brown*. Frank has also produced four movies, including the Emmy Award-

Photo credit: Matt Copping

winning NBC movie *Babe Ruth*. This is the third book he has co-authored, the first two with Rod Carew and Armen Keteyian. *If These Lips Could Talk* is the first of three he has co-written with author Billy O'Connor.

Billy O'Connor

Born in County Cork Ireland, Billy O'Connor grew up on the Bronx streets. After Vietnam, Billy was a teamster, a pub and restaurant owner, and a New York City firefighter for twenty proud years. He was also an illegal bookmaker. Billy lived this eclectic life despite his addiction to drugs and alcohol.

Courtesy of Bill O'Connor

After the tragedy of 9/11 and the loss of 343 of his brother firefighters, Billy sobered up and attended the University of Florida. At the age of sixty-two, he earned his journalism degree and began to write and perform stand-up comedy. His first book, Confessions of a *Bronx Bookie*, was published to wide acclaim in 2015.

INDEX